LONG STORY SHORT

LONG STORY SHORT

AN ANTHOLOGY OF (MOSTLY) 10-MINUTE PLAYS

EDITED BY REBECCA BURTON

PLAYWRIGHTS CANADA PRESS
TORONTO

LIBRARY AND ARCHIVES CANADA CATALOGUING IN PUBLICATION

Long story short : an anthology of (mostly) 10-minute plays / edited by Rebecca Burton.

ISBN 978-1-77091-563-3 (paperback)

1. Ten-minute plays. 2. One-act plays, Canadian (English). 3. Canadian drama--21st century. I. Burton, Rebecca Lyn, 1969-, editor

PS8309.O5L66 2016   C812'.0410806   C2016-906698-3

We acknowledge the financial support of the Canada Council for the Arts, the Ontario Arts Council (OAC), the Ontario Media Development Corporation, and the Government of Canada through the Canada Book Fund for our publishing activities. Nous remercions l'appui financier du Conseil des Arts du Canada, le Conseil arts de l'Ontario (CAO), la Société de développement de l'industrie des médias de l'Ontario, et le Gouvernement du Canada par l'entremise du Fonds du livre du Canada pour nos activités d'édition.

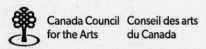

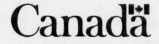

LONG STORY SHORT

Contents

A Little Something for Everyone:
Introducing *Long Story Short*

I am excited to introduce this unique collection of (mostly) ten-minute plays. It was inspired in large part by the desire to help fill a void, for while there are a number of short play anthologies and dedicated websites in existence currently, none offer specifically Canadian content or authorship. Playwrights Canada Press published *Instant Applause: Twenty-Nine Very Short Complete Plays* (2004), a compilation of works culled from Blizzard Press's two volumes of *Instant Applause* (1994, 1996), but those editions are out of print now, leaving a noticeable gap in the field. This is a burgeoning art form; certainly it's time for a new volume. The ten-minute play format has increased in popularity, as evidenced by the growth of contests, festivals, and programming as part of regular theatre seasons. There are a number of reasons for the mounting attraction: short plays are economical, often requiring minimal design elements and technical support; they offer a multiplicity of roles and learning opportunities for actors and other practitioners; they provide a diversity of experiences for a variety of spectators; and they present complete worlds in truncated form, which requires a precision and deftness of craft that appeals to professional companies, amateur and community theatres, as well as high school, college, and university theatre departments. It is my hope that *Long Story Short* will serve all of these communities, and as wide an audience as possible, by offering up a fresh infusion of Canadian work for all to enjoy.

Notions of "general appeal" and "accessibility" (in the broadest sense of the term) guided my play-selection process, and in an effort to compile a collection for all occasions and a variety of tastes, the works included here are intended to represent collectively an assortment of styles. Thus, there is an array of genres ranging from historical period piece (*Flesh Offerings*) to futuristic dystopia (*The Prisoner*), from swash-buckling Hollywood tale (*The Baited Blade*) to Jazz-based monodrama (*Steps*), from light comedy (*The Living Library*) to classical revisionism (*Sisters*), and from absurdist drama (*Cook*) to feminist satire (*Say The Words*), to name but a few. The selected plays also offer various actor configurations, such as solo shows and two-handers, threesomes and foursomes, and a work that expands cast size beyond the norm by integrating the audience. To further strengthen the anthology's allure, the collection incorporates a variety of themes. Some plays feature centuries-old topics, such as coming-of-age (*The Book of Daniel*), love (*Nancy*), heartbreak (*It's Gonna Be a Bright*), family relations (*Summer's End*), god and (wo)man (*Garbed in Flesh*), and death (*Brother, Brother, The Auction, Troupe*). Others present contemporary takes on issues specific to modern society, such as coming out (*Friend for Life, This Isn't Toronto*), gender norms (*Burusera, Pee & Qs*), racialized relations (*A Recipe for Tomato Butter, The Only Good Indian*), and environmental concerns (*Air Apparent, An Ordinary Man, Green Dating*).

It was personally and politically important to me that this collection boast an equitable balance of playwrights by gender, as women often find themselves marginalized in and sometimes excluded from anthologies. I also wanted to ensure that the works offered a number of roles for women (since they face fewer performance opportunities), and substantial roles at that (given that female characters often serve as adjuncts to men), preferably with a variety of age ranges (not just the ingenue or mother figure). I believe these goals were met. Of the twenty-five plays contained herein, thirteen (52%) are written by women, eleven (44%) by men, and one (4%) by a combination of the two; as it turns out, the figures are in keeping with the number of women and men who submitted plays for consideration.

After sifting through the numbers related to gender and authorship, I was curious to see how the play selections stacked up statistically in other respects. While the anthology succeeds with gender equity, it utterly fails when it comes to representations of disability (aside from a character with a lisp in *Brother, Brother*). Nor does it do well in terms of ethno-cultural diversity: only three plays are written by an Indigenous playwright (*Flesh Offerings*) or person of colour (*Say the Words* and *The Only Good Indian*). Dismayed by the latter discovery, I examined the submission rates again, this time to see if an unintended bias influenced my selection process and contributed to the low numbers. Approximately 6% of the play submissions were written by people of colour or Indigenous folks, compared to 12% of the anthology's works. Though the figure is doubled, it is woefully inadequate for a collection intended to appeal to a large segment of society. This finding suggests that an open call issued via traditional channels is not sufficient. Changes need to be made in relation to how and where notices are circulated, so that a greater diversity of people have an opportunity to respond. While the absence of people of colour and Indigenous playwrights is highly problematic, the severity of underrepresentation can be mitigated somewhat in performance. Four plays require specific ethno-cultural casting choices (*The Only Good Indian*, *Flesh Offerings*, the Jewish-themed *The Book of Daniel*, and *Troupe*, which is set in the Ukraine), but the others do not dictate nationality or skin colour, and some pointedly encourage diverse casting practices (*Air Apparent*, *The Prisoner*). As a result, there are greater opportunities than it might seem for embodying multiplicities and cultural pluralism.

Much to my surprise, the anthology's greatest imbalance occurs in relation to the playwrights' regional affiliations. I was shocked to discover that eighteen (or 72%!) of the authors I chose currently reside in Ontario (eleven or 44% live in Toronto), five (20%) are situated in other provinces, and two (8%) live outside of Canada. When I assessed the submissions in relation to region, I found that 56% of the plays were written by people living in Ontario (29% of those by Toronto-dwellers), 37.5% were penned by people in other provinces, and 6.5% were crafted by individuals living abroad. I did not consciously consider where the playwrights lived during my selection process, but clearly I should have. The figures expose an undeniable partiality for plays written in my home province; a bias that I was unaware of before undertaking this project, but one that I will most certainly safeguard against in the future.

Despite these imbalances, it is my hope that there truly is a little something for everyone in these pages. There is no one overriding concept, style, or scope that permeates the collection, yet each play included here has the ability to travel from the page into the hearts and minds of audiences and readers alike. These ten-minute plays moved me, as I hope they will you, with their displays of humanity in all its facets and glory, effectively rendering a long story short.

The Book of Daniel
by Lawrence Aronovitch

A man recalls his days as a Jewish high school student in Montreal in the 1970s when he used the reasoning skills his teachers taught him to argue that they should stop pushing him to date girls. A story about not coming out until you're ready.

The Book of Daniel was produced at the New Theatre of Ottawa in November of 2013 with the following cast and creative team:

Daniel	Eric Craig
Mrs. Cohen	Maureen Smith
Rabbi Stern	Brian K. Stewart
Director	John Koensgen
Costumes	Vanessa Imeson
Lighting	Sean Green, Martin Conboy
Sound	Jon Carter
Set	John Doucet

CHARACER LIST

Daniel	fourteen years old
Mrs. Cohen	a teacher
Rabbi Stern	another teacher

A NOTE ON THE TEXT

The story is told from the point of view of the adult Daniel in the present day.

...

Lawrence Aronovitch was born in Montreal and went on to study history and physics at Harvard University. This led to a satisfying career in the US space program and then an invitation from the Canadian government to come home and help start up the Canadian Space Agency.

After a few more twists and turns, Lawrence began to write plays in 2007. A former playwright-in-residence at the Great Canadian Theatre Company, Lawrence is currently working with Ottawa's Bear & Co. on a new play about an elderly tailor.

The Book of Daniel

DANIEL   *(out)* So here's the thing. It's Montreal. Nineteen seventy-six. The Olympics are coming. I can't wait.

MRS. COHEN   Danny, you're a good boy, but you know what? Mathematics is never going to be your strong suit. That's fine. Lots of people get through life without mastering the finer points of trigonometry.

DANIEL   Thanks for the vote of confidence, Mrs. Cohen. *(out)* Mrs. Cohen, she's my math teacher. I'm fourteen years old and I'm failing in math.

MRS. COHEN   But the problem, Danny, is that you're failing in math. What's the matter, darling? Girls on your mind?

DANIEL   *(out)* Like I say, it's 1976. Math teachers can still call you darling. Especially when they're best friends with—

MRS. COHEN   Your mother is worried about you, Danny. You're not like the other boys.

DANIEL   She really wants me to get drunk, throw up, and total the car?

MRS. COHEN   No, of course not, darling. She just wants what's best for you. But you stay home all the time and you don't seem to go out with your friends.

DANIEL   The other students here aren't exactly my friends, Mrs. Cohen.

MRS. COHEN   You remember Sammy Schwartz, don't you? He was two years ahead of you. He didn't like to socialize either. But at least it was because he studied. You know where he is now?

DANIEL   *(out)* Harvard.

MRS. COHEN   He's at Harvard. He's going to be a somebody. And you know why?

DANIEL   Because he studied?

MRS. COHEN   Exactly. I don't think your mother would mind your staying in all the time if you at least studied. But what do you do all day? She says you're reading comic books.

DANIEL   You can learn a lot from comic books, Mrs. Cohen. I'll bet Sammy Schwartz read comic books. I'll bet that's how he got into Harvard.

MRS. COHEN   I can't believe you'd think such a thing. Comic books. I can see the writing on the wall now— you'll read your comic books and fail your studies and your poor mother, do you know what she'll say then?

DANIEL   You're going to tell me, aren't you.

MRS. COHEN   Tell you? Of course I'm going to tell you. She'll say I failed you, Danny. That we all failed you. So listen to me, darling. No more comic books, okay? Try a little math instead. And you need to get out more.

DANIEL   *(out)* So this was her logic. I need to study more but at the same time I need to get out more to assuage my mother's worries, which were now Mrs. Cohen's worries too, that I'm not socializing with my peers. So how do I reconcile the two? Easy. I talk to Rabbi Stern.

RABBI STERN	Daniel. Come in, my boy, come in. What's on your mind today?
DANIEL	*(out)* This is how he always greeted me. "What's on your mind?" Not "How are you." Not "What's new." But "What's on your mind?" It's a rabbinical way of saying hello, I guess.
RABBI STERN	Mrs. Cohen has been talking about you again, Daniel.
DANIEL	*(out)* See, the thing I loved about him was that he called me Daniel. Which is my name. Not Danny. Which is what Mrs. Cohen calls me. And my mother.
RABBI STERN	She says you're not studying hard enough at math.
DANIEL	She says she sees the writing on the wall.
RABBI STERN	Really? And what do you suppose she means by that?
DANIEL	If she means the graffiti next to the main entrance, that wasn't me.
RABBI STERN	It's an expression, Daniel. From the Bible. Which you would know if you paid a little more attention in my class, never mind Mrs. Cohen's. It means you've been weighed in the balance and found wanting.
DANIEL	Weighed in the balance? Sounds like a math problem. No wonder Mrs. Cohen likes the expression.
RABBI STERN	You're a smart boy, Daniel. You use your head. Now if you could only use it a little bit for Mrs. Cohen's class.
DANIEL	*(out)* What I see now, is that he respected me. By calling me Daniel. That's important when you're fourteen—well, at any age, I guess. No other teacher in our little Jewish school did that. And because he respected me, he was someone I could go and talk to. About anything.

RABBI STERN — No one expects you to be a genius at every subject, of course, but you need to at least put in an effort. Education is a very important thing. Even trigonometry.

DANIEL — *(out)* Well, almost anything. Rabbi Stern was a master of Talmudic logic, yes, so he could probably help me deal with Mrs. Cohen and my mother worrying about my study habits. Usually this meant that he answered questions by asking other questions. But what would he have to say to me about girls?

MRS. COHEN — I don't know what to do, Rabbi. He's not a bad student. But he keeps getting the quizzes wrong. With the school year almost over, I would hate for him to fail the course. And I would hate for his mother to worry. You know what she can be like.

RABBI STERN — And do you have any ideas about why he might be in such an unfortunate position?

MRS. COHEN — Girls. I'm sure it has to do with girls.

RABBI STERN — Well, he is at that age, you know.

MRS. COHEN — So what am I supposed to do?

RABBI STERN — Who says you're supposed to do anything?

MRS. COHEN — His mother.

RABBI STERN — And what is it that his mother wants you to do? Get his mind off girls?

MRS. COHEN — Actually, she wishes his mind would be a little more on girls and a little less on comic books.

RABBI STERN — I'll agree that a boy his age really shouldn't be spending so much of his time on comic books. Still, it isn't exactly what I would call a grave sin.

MRS. COHEN — And thinking about girls?

RABBI STERN — Really, Mrs. Cohen, is that such a terrible thing either?

MRS. COHEN — Yes, if it's interfering with his studying.

RABBI STERN	I suspect girls have been interfering with boys' studying since Moses parted the Red Sea, if not before. It's perfectly natural.
MRS. COHEN	Surely you wouldn't condone—
RABBI STERN	No, of course not. But one must make allowances for youth. We can't expect our students to be angels, Mrs. Cohen.
MRS. COHEN	Is that what you tell your class?
RABBI STERN	Well, when the Bible gets to who begat whom, let's just say that I don't feel the need to focus on the mechanics of the begats in class.
MRS. COHEN	I think they already know the mechanics, Rabbi.
RABBI STERN	Perhaps. But if they do, they learned it from Mrs. Shield, the biology teacher. Not from me.
MRS. COHEN	And do you suggest, Rabbi, that we ask Danny to consult with Mrs. Shield as well?
RABBI STERN	Well, Mrs. Cohen, that depends. Do you feel that what the boy needs is a lesson in biology or in the art of human relationships?
MRS. COHEN	He looks up to you, Rabbi, that's all I'm saying. Mrs. Shield, not so much. And me, I know I just remind him of his mother.
RABBI STERN	So he needs a father figure in his life, is this what you're saying?
MRS. COHEN	I think he does, yes.
DANIEL	*(out)* Well, I suppose Mrs. Cohen had a point. My father died when I was little. I'm sure he was a good man, but I never really knew him. If someone was going to fill that role, why not Rabbi Stern?
MRS. COHEN	After all, you know what they say . . .
DANIEL	*(out)* But mainly I think Mrs. Cohen was worried I might turn into too much of a mama's boy.
RABBI STERN	I'll talk to him, Mrs. Cohen. I'll talk to him.

DANIEL	*(out)* So it's almost summer, and I'm looking forward to the Olympics. It's all I can think about. I figure it's as close as I'll ever get to people who can run faster than a speeding bullet or leap tall buildings in a single bound. Rabbi Stern asks to see me. I don't know why. Maybe he's interested in the Olympics too? I don't think so. It's not in the Bible, is it?
RABBI STERN	Daniel, my boy. Come in, come in. What's on your mind today?
DANIEL	Um, you are, Rabbi. You wanted to see me?
RABBI STERN	Oh, yes, that's right. *(beat)* You know, Daniel, it's not easy being your age.
DANIEL	Is this about Mrs. Cohen and my mother?
RABBI STERN	I beg your pardon?
DANIEL	They're worried about girls.
RABBI STERN	Girls? Who said anything about girls?
DANIEL	Mrs. Cohen put you up to this, didn't she. She wants you to talk to me about girls.
RABBI STERN	Well—
DANIEL	I know about girls, Rabbi.
RABBI STERN	I'm sure you do. It's just that she's worried about your studies.
DANIEL	Let me ask you something, Rabbi. When you were my age, were you worrying about girls? Was your mother worrying about you worrying about girls?

A *pause.*

Rabbi?

RABBI STERN	Who said we were talking about girls?
DANIEL	Mrs. Cohen is talking about girls. My mother is talking about girls. Everyone, it seems, is talking about girls. So I figure, why not you too? Me, I don't really feel the need to talk about girls, thank

you very much. The new Superman comic, now *that* I'm happy to talk about.

RABBI STERN   All right. You know, Daniel, there's nothing wrong with talking about girls.

DANIEL   Well, okay. But would you agree that there's nothing wrong with *not* talking about girls?

RABBI STERN   Mrs. Cohen's concerned about your quizzes, that's all. She thinks it might be because you're thinking about girls. Most boys do, so she thought—

DANIEL   You're not listening to what I'm saying, Rabbi. Didn't you tell me never to do something just because everybody does it? Aren't I supposed to think for myself? Be my own man? You taught me that. For my bar mitzvah. You think I've forgotten?

RABBI STERN   You're right. That's what I taught you.

DANIEL   And you also taught me not to judge other people if I didn't know why they made the decisions they did. So please don't tell me I'm supposed to think about girls because everyone else in class is. And don't tell me not to think about my comic books if that's what I want to do. Please?

RABBI STERN   We just want to make sure you're all right, that's all.

DANIEL   I'm fine. Except that I feel like I'm being judged if I don't do what you or Mrs. Cohen or my mother think I should be doing.

RABBI STERN   Your mother named you well, you know.

DANIEL   What does my name have to do with anything?

RABBI STERN   Daniel. It means "God is my judge."

Beat.

You know what? You're absolutely right. We should leave it to Him to judge, not ourselves.

DANIEL   Maybe you could you explain that to my mother? And Mrs. Cohen too?

RABBI STERN   You mustn't be so hard on them. They're concerned about you, that's all.

DANIEL   Why is everyone so concerned about me?

RABBI STERN   That's what people do when they care for you, Daniel.

DANIEL   Was everyone concerned for you when you were my age, Rabbi Stern?

A *pause.*

RABBI STERN   That's a difficult question to answer.

DANIEL   Well, I just think sometimes that you teachers forget what it's like to be young.

RABBI STERN   I'm sure that's not true.

DANIEL   I am. If you remembered, you'd see why I'd rather talk about my comic books. Did you have Superman growing up?

RABBI STERN   I don't like to think about it, Daniel.

DANIEL   Why?

RABBI STERN   You ask that question a lot, Daniel.

DANIEL   Just like you taught me.

RABBI STERN   Mrs. Cohen should be so lucky.

DANIEL   So? What were you doing when you were my age?

RABBI STERN   Sit down, Daniel.

DANIEL sits.

                When I was your age, I was living in Shanghai.

DANIEL   No, really? That's so cool. Like the movie?

RABBI STERN   What movie?

DANIEL   *The Lady from Shanghai.* Orson Welles. It's an amazing movie. Rita Hayworth. She plays this mysterious woman and there's this yacht and there's supposed to be this murder—

RABBI STERN   It wasn't like *The Lady from Shanghai*, Daniel.

DANIEL	No?
RABBI STERN	It's where I lived for a time. After I had to leave Vienna.
DANIEL	Oh.
RABBI STERN	It was not a happy time. I don't like to dwell on it.

Beat.

DANIEL	Yeah. I guess you weren't thinking about Superman then. Or trigonometry or girls.
RABBI STERN	No. You know, I met many people in my travels in those days. Some of them did extraordinary things. Some good, some not so good. That's when I learned how hard it is to judge someone for what they decide to do. You can't always know the reason for it.
DANIEL	Okay.
RABBI STERN	I also learned that you have to take responsibility for the choices you make. So that you are not weighed in the balance and found wanting. That's very important, Daniel. Do you understand?
DANIEL	I think so.
RABBI STERN	You're a good boy, Daniel. Be good to your mother. And even to Mrs. Cohen. If you want to focus on Superman just now, that's fine. If you don't want to think about girls just now, well, that's fine too. It's your choice. Nobody should judge you for that.
DANIEL	Thank you, Rabbi.
RABBI STERN	But please, Daniel. Trigonometry. Don't fail the course. Okay?
DANIEL	*(out)* So here's the thing. Last week I got an email from the school. The alumni office. Usually they're looking for a donation, but this time it was to tell me that Rabbi Stern had died. He was a good man. That spring before the Olympics, that was the first time he told me about Shanghai.

When I was older, he told me more. It was a terrible time. Like he said, some people had to do extraordinary things, some good, some not so good. Including him. I think he always feared being weighed in the balance and found wanting. But who am I to judge. And me? I passed trigonometry. I had fun at the Olympics. And I grew up. Sold my comic books on eBay. I made some smart choices. And some dumb ones. On balance, I hope, I made my mother proud. And Rabbi Stern too. And you know what? He was as good as his word. Never judged me. And he never stopped calling me Daniel.

CURTAIN

The Baited Blade
by David Belke

In the golden age of motion pictures one of the world's most successful movie stars visits a veteran character actor in order to receive lessons in swordsmanship. But as past sins are revisited, what started out as a bitter rivalry transforms into a suspenseful duel not only of blades, but also wits, nerve, and deception.

The Baited Blade was produced by P3 Productions at the Edmonton Fringe Theatre Festival (part of *Klang! Pow! Kersplat! The Fight Show*), directed by Troy O'Donnell and featuring the following cast and creative team:

Quentin Woodrow	Kyle Jorde
Alex Witt	Garett Ross
Margaret	Melissa Hande

Stage Manager	Elizabeth Allison
Fight Choreography by the company	Troy O'Donnell, Kyle Jorde, Garett Ross, Melissa Hande, and Rachel Johnstone

CHARACTER LIST

Quentin Woodrow	actor, known for playing villainous parts, elegant, English (late forties)
Alex Witt	actor, known for playing heroes and swashbucklers, Australian, light accent (midthirties)
Margaret	housekeeper, silent, sphinx-like (twenties)

SETTING
The parlour in the mansion of Quentin Woodrow, Hollywood, late 1930s. A dark and rainy autumn night.

...

David Belke's first full-length play was produced for the 1990 Edmonton Fringe Theatre Festival, and in the years since he has written a new play for each subsequent festival becoming one the Fringe's mainstays and one of the city's favourite playwrights.

A multiple Sterling Award–winner, David has seen over fifty of his plays professionally produced over the course of his career. His work has been seen across Canada, as well as in the United States, England, Northern Ireland, India, Ghana, and Greece. David's celebrated comedy, *That Darn Plot*, received the Samuel French Inc. Canadian Playwright Award in 2000.

Active in Edmonton's theatre community, David has served as the Northern Alberta representative for the National Council of the Playwrights Guild of Canada and co-created Script Salon, Edmonton's nationally recognized monthly play-reading series.

Although playwriting occupies the wobbly centre of his life, David has performed many different roles in the theatre world. He's an actor, a designer, an improviser, a director, a voice actor, and a teacher. But offstage he is best known to thousands of school kids all over Edmonton simply as Mr. Belke.

The Baited Blade

The parlour of QUENTIN *Woodrow. The room is big and gothically elegant, large enough to suggest a castle or a Hollywood mansion of which it is the latter. A phonograph plays something appropriately dramatic. There is a great deal of open space, because the furniture has been cleared away or pushed to the side. What remains are an armchair or two and a large, intricately carved table.*

It is a dark and stormy night, of course.

MARGARET *enters carrying a tray with a brandy decanter and two snifters. She sets it on the table. She is dressed in a style that suggests, though by no means duplicates, the uniform of a house domestic. Impassive and stoic, she gives every appearance of being the typical servant.*

QUENTIN *Woodrow enters. He is an older man though whippet, fit, and elegant. He projects an air of sardonic culture and cerebral exactitude. He takes in the room.*

There is a door chime. MARGARET *turns to* QUENTIN *for confirmation. He nods. She exits.* QUENTIN *turns off the music. He takes a deep breath in preparation and checks his jacket pocket. Ready. He arranges himself carefully, finally choosing a pose by the liquor.*

ALEX Witt enters. He's a young screen idol, handsome with a raffish air about him. He is dressed flawlessly in fashion, although he looks a little dishevelled thanks to the soaking of rain.

MARGARET, having just let him in, follows.

ALEX	Quentin!
QUENTIN	Alex. Do come in. Why don't you get out of that wet coat and catch your breath?
ALEX	Yes. Good. Thanks. I've been looking forward to this all day. *(MARGARET helps ALEX off with his coat.)* Thanks, luv. *(really seeing her)* Well, well. Look at you. Thought it would just be the old man and me. Nice to have a pretty face to liven things up.

He winks and throws her an award-winning smile. MARGARET's face remains an impassive mask. She exits with the coat.

	(smiling knowingly) She lives here?
QUENTIN	In the servant's quarters.
ALEX	Quite young to be the housekeeper.
QUENTIN	She has other duties.
ALEX	*(salacious)* You old dog. I didn't think you had it in you. *(laughs)*
QUENTIN	Ah. You think— Of course you would. Well, it's not quite like that.
ALEX	It never is. Might one have a drink before starting things off?
QUENTIN	Are you sure that's wise? *(goes to decanter, pours two drinks)*
ALEX	I'm going to need one if I'm going to get through this. I'm soaked to the skin and it was murder on set. Curtiz *(pronounced Kur-teez)* barking orders at me all day. And then on top of all that I had to meet with the lawyers again.

QUENTIN	*(delivering the drink)* Lawyers?
ALEX	Damn nuisance. But that's the price of fame, I suppose.
QUENTIN	I suppose so. *(toast)* Price of fame.
ALEX	Price of fame. *(throwing back the drink)* Another?
QUENTIN	*(not drinking)* Are you sure? There are serious consequences for error tonight. This isn't play.
ALEX	It'll help ease the tension. *(After a moment QUENTIN passes ALEX his own glass, and he returns the empty snifter to the tray.)* I really appreciate you doing this for me.
QUENTIN	I must admit to a little surprise. Surely you've had some lessons in swordplay.
ALEX	Pirates and knights. When you work with broadsword it's mostly just slash and hack. I can fake that well enough. So, no. No lessons beyond the basics.
QUENTIN	I never would have known.
ALEX	Acting hides a lot of ignorance. But now there's this musketeer movie. You can't just hack away at things.
QUENTIN	I imagine you must have some natural ability.
ALEX	Everything's natural. Never had any plan to be an actor. I was just some truck driver from Bondi *(pronounced Bond-eye).* But then some guy decides I got a look and, boom, I'm a movie star.
QUENTIN	When you have the right look . . .
ALEX	My agent calls my face the million-dollar mug.
QUENTIN	Sounds like an agent. So you've never studied at all? Not even after you became an actor?
ALEX	Is that a problem?
QUENTIN	Just like to know what I have to work with. I, on the other hand, studied all my life. I grew up on the stage. Dedicated myself to my craft. My art.

ALEX   And that's why you're the best in the biz. Though it's kind of kind of funny, isn't it?

QUENTIN   What is?

ALEX   You're the best swordsman in Hollywood.

QUENTIN   Yes.

ALEX   But onscreen you never get to win a fight. Sort of funny, isn't it?

QUENTIN   The price of a villainous physiognomy. It wins me parts, but I know I'll never play the hero. Winning is for the Alex Witts of the world. *(taking* ALEX's *glass)* Shall we begin?

ALEX   Ready when you are.

QUENTIN   Very good. *(He rings a bell, takes off his jacket.)* You said you were meeting with lawyers?

ALEX   Studio lawyers. Just another fan thing. Some girl looking for attention.

QUENTIN   And that requires lawyers?

ALEX   Same old story. Meet a pretty thing. Have a good time. Then instead of letting go, she tries to take a piece of you. Price of fame.

QUENTIN   Price of fame. And of course you're especially vulnerable. Ever since Santa Monica.

ALEX   That was years ago. Not even worth bringing up.

QUENTIN   The things done by one of us reflects on all of us. I was here when the whole Fatty Arbuckle affair arose. Nearly brought down the entire industry. And the sad fact is that poor Roscoe was crucified for something he didn't do. While so many never have to pay for the things they most certainly did do. Funny ol' business.

ALEX   Yes. Funny. *(beat)* You really don't like me very much do you?

QUENTIN   *(casually)* No. Can't say as I do.

MARGARET enters. She carries two pairs of gloves and a number of fencing blades in the crook of her arm. She arranges them on the table. QUENTIN *crosses to the weapons.*

Ah. Here we are. The weapons in question. These are all from my own private collection. *(examines the weapons)* There are three basic weapons in fencing. The foil: designed for use in training. But considering your vast hacking and slashing experience, I think we can move on to something a little more advanced. Sabre: originally used a cavalry weapon. It is heavier and thicker. But not really what you would call a musketeer's weapon. A little crude. Not terribly elegant. A weapon of attack. *(casually)* Whatever happened to that girl?

ALEX   I'm sorry?

QUENTIN   Santa Monica. Whatever happened to her?

ALEX   I really don't know. Can't say I care. I'm sorry I ever met that honeytrap.

QUENTIN   Come now. It was hardly her fault. She was underage after all. Innocent in the ways of the world. What was her name now? Betty Ann? Peggy Sue? Some farm-girl name.

ALEX   *(temper growing)* Look. As far as I'm concerned, it's over and done with. I was plastered and I can't be held responsible for my actions. That's what the courts said. I'm sorry you old-timers feel like I've put you out, but it's finished. All right?

QUENTIN   *(beat)* I think we'll concentrate on épée tonight. *(gestures to* MARGARET, *she gives* ALEX *his gloves and blade)* The épée has no edge. Note the flexibility of the blade. This demands—

ALEX   What about strategy? How do I fight with this?

QUENTIN   The strategy is the same in every bout. Slip through the opponent's defences and drive in the point. That is the only way you can win in this game.

ALEX   Right.

QUENTIN   This blade may not seem very dangerous, but keep in mind with the entire weight of a fully grown adult concentrated behind the épée's tip it is fully capable of puncturing steel or splitting human bone. That's not to mention the potential scarring.

ALEX   Then shouldn't we have some sort of protection? Masks or something?

QUENTIN   Worried about that million-dollar mug?

ALEX   Shouldn't I?

QUENTIN   Come now. This is only a lesson. And besides, the blades have been baited.

ALEX   Baited?

QUENTIN   Blunted. Little stoppers attached to the tips. See. *(pushing his palm against the tip and making the blade bend)* Harmless. Now. The first thing we shall have to master is the grip. You must balance—

ALEX   I think I've got it. *(makes an impressive flourish with the blade)* I *do* have the basics after all.

QUENTIN   So you do.

ALEX   I want to move on to the fancy stuff.

QUENTIN   *(beat)* Fancy stuff it shall be then.

MARGARET takes an observer's position. QUENTIN and ALEX take up opposite positions.

When you enter a sword fight you are accountable not only for your own safety, but that of your partner as well. Try to exercise a little responsibility for once in your life. *(ALEX seethes.)* You lead with your right foot. The left foot is at a right angle as you can see. You move forward pushing from your left. This allows you to close the distance between your opponent.

ALEX   Like this?

ALEX lunges forward. QUENTIN steps back from the unexpected attack and parries. There is a flurry of blades before they break. The two carefully regard each other from a distance.

QUENTIN   I suppose we mark that down as youthful enthusiasm.

ALEX   I just wanted to show you what I've got.

QUENTIN   Shall we return to the lesson?

ALEX   You with all your training and skills. It doesn't matter a bit.

QUENTIN   We should cover attacks—

ALEX   I'm the bloody hero.

QUENTIN   —and deflections.

ALEX   I may never have been able to afford acting classes and I may never have had your chances, but I do all right. I have talent, mate. Natural talent. And charisma. And those are things puffed-up antiques like you and your kind will never have, never learn, and never buy.

QUENTIN   At least we can keep our zippers up. Mate.

ALEX   It's time someone put you toffs in your place.

QUENTIN   Then *(En garde stance)* come.

ALEX rushes in. It is a furious attack, both men enraged; QUENTIN is more skilled and demonstrates more technique, but ALEX is driven by youth and anger. It is a wildly physical, see-saw battle. MARGARET watches impassively.

ALEX   Ready to say it?

QUENTIN   What?

ALEX   I'm just as good as you.

QUENTIN   Hardly.

The fight continues. QUENTIN manages to get some painful blows in with the side of his blade, but ALEX fights through. The fight pauses for a moment. ALEX holds his arm in pain.

You seem to have something more than the basics, my friend.

ALEX   Some, yeah.

QUENTIN   So why ask for a lesson?

ALEX   I didn't say I was the one who needed to be taught a lesson.

Fight. Fast and furious. Both men have something to prove. They find themselves in a clinch.

How does it feel, Quentin? You can't beat the man with no training. I may not be an artist—

QUENTIN   Jesus!

ALEX   —but I know what I can do. And right now—

QUENTIN   For Christ's sake, stop this. *(QUENTIN violently pushes ALEX away.)*

ALEX   *(stepping forward with blade)* What are you—

QUENTIN   Stop it. Drop it. Do you want to get us both killed? *(drops his blade)*

ALEX   What? What are—

QUENTIN   For God's sake. Just look at your blade. It's become unbaited. There's a real point on that thing.

ALEX   *(dumbly looks at the blade)* Oh, God.

QUENTIN   *(snatching the blade from ALEX)* It could have gone through an eye. The heart. And you, running around like a maniac with no regard—

ALEX   God. *(beat)* I need a drink.

ALEX and QUENTIN cross to the decanter together. They simultaneously reach for the bottle and their hands collide. They look at each other.

BOTH   Jesus.

There is a frozen moment and then QUENTIN stifles a chuckle. ALEX releases a chortle. Soon the two are laughing together. ALEX pours a drink. QUENTIN regards the unbaited blade.

QUENTIN	We were close to bloodshed. How this blade ever lost its stopper . . .
ALEX	When I think what could've happened . . .
QUENTIN	Let's be thankful that the only thing we accomplished was wearing each other out.
ALEX	*(pouring)* And some bruises. You're fast with that blade, old man. *(drinks)* Maybe we should end the lesson. Before we stick each other in the gut.
QUENTIN	*(lays the unbaited blade across the armchair)* The first part. We'll end the first part of the lesson.
ALEX	Thanks. My heart is pounding like a rabbit's. I'm worn out.
QUENTIN	*(putting on his jacket)* Then we should move on to the second part.
ALEX	Really, Quentin. I think we should just call it a night.
QUENTIN	Not yet. I'd like you to meet another one of my students.
ALEX	Quentin, please.
QUENTIN	Margaret has been studying with me for years. Why don't you offer us a demonstration, my dear?

MARGARET has crossed to the table and picked up a weapon. She runs through some impressive exercises and demonstrations as QUENTIN talks.

	She came to me. Looking for lessons. Like you, she heard I was the best. And having come into some money, she too could afford the best. But after I heard her story, I was more than pleased to take her on for free. There was a certain poetry to the matter that appealed to me.
ALEX	I'm not exactly sure what I'm supposed to be getting out of this, Quentin.
QUENTIN	It's a lesson, Alex. A lesson in strategy. Slip through the opponent's defences and drive in the

point. That is the only way you can win in this game.

ALEX   Quentin—

QUENTIN   She has been with me for years now. We've gotten to know each other quite well. But I suppose it is the old manners in me that keeps calling her Margaret. Her family was much more informal. They called her Peggy Ann.

The point of MARGARET's *blade suddenly stops in front of* ALEX's *throat. He freezes.*

ALEX   Christ.

QUENTIN   I suppose it's only natural that you wouldn't recognize her. It was a number of years ago after all. And you have been doing your level best to blot her from your memory. But she remembers. She remembers everything.

ALEX   I'm going now. I don't have to—

QUENTIN   *(removing a pistol from his jacket)* Oh, I think you must. As I was saying, Margaret's memories are quite clear. And I think she would take some issue with the whole thing being her fault. Oh, you were plastered, that's true. But she is of the firm opinion that you forced yourself on her.

ALEX   What do you want?

QUENTIN   One more bout. You and her. Then we'll call it a night.

ALEX   A fight, another fight? After you wore me out and poured all that booze down my throat?

QUENTIN   Although I take credit for the former, you more than amply took care of the latter yourself. All I mean to do now is make sure you stay and defend your honour. Although I could hardly think of a more sorry prize.

ALEX   *(to* MARGARET*)* So you're going to put me my place now? You're going to prove you're better than me? All right. If that's what it takes to settle this thing, then let's get this over with. *(MARGARET crosses to ALEX and gives him her blade.)* But just remember. When all this is done, I'm still going home the hero. I'm still the hero.

Without taking her eyes off ALEX, MARGARET holds out her hand. QUENTIN gives her the unbaited blade.

Quentin. What are you—? Quentin, that's—

QUENTIN   You'll have to be careful, Alex. An unbaited blade *can* leave a very deep and nasty scar. More than enough to discount that million-dollar mug of yours. I really don't think she means to kill you. But the truth of the matter is, I really don't know what she is planning. But I suppose we'll all find out soon enough. Shall we begin?

ALEX is helpless, the sword hangs limply in his hand, he looks at MARGARET with dread.

MARGARET   *(settling into her stance with a vicious smile)* En garde.

Blackout.

Green Dating
A play
by Chantal Bilodeau

A teenage girl with very specific ideas about what she wants in a man makes it clear she won't settle for someone who doesn't meet her environmental standards.

Green Dating was originally read in The Movement Theatre Company's Go Green event in New York City on April 29, 2009. It premiered in Manhattan Theatre Source's EstroGenius Festival in New York City on October 19–22, 2011. Barbara Harrison directed the following cast:

Girl   Quinn Warren
Boy   Eugene Oh

CHARACTER LIST
A teenage girl
A teenage boy

SETTING
A street corner. Now.

...

Chantal Bilodeau is a New York playwright and translator originally from Montreal. She is the artistic director of The Arctic Cycle—an organization created to support the writing, development, and production of eight plays that look at the massive social and environmental changes taking place in the eight countries of the Arctic—and the founder of the blog and international network Artists And Climate Change. She was a co-organizer of Climate Change Theatre Action, which presented one hundred events in twenty-six countries in support of the United Nations 2015 Paris Climate Conference.

Her plays have been presented across the US, Canada, Mexico, and Norway. She is the recipient of a Woodward International Playwriting Prize as well as first prize in the Earth Matters on Stage Ecodrama Festival and the Uprising National Playwriting Competition. She has been in residence at the Banff Centre and the National Theatre School of Canada and is published by Talonbooks.

Visit her at www.cbilodeau.com, www.thearcticcycle.org, and www.artistsandclimatechange.com.

Green Dating

A street corner. Two teenagers, their tongues down each other's throats, making out like nobody's business. After a beat, the GIRL *comes up for air.*

GIRL   Wow. I mean fuck, it's like, you know?

BOY   Yeah.

GIRL   Like this, I don't know, this, I mean I hope I don't freak you out but I'm like completely like . . . WOW.

BOY   I hear ya. I mean this is like totally fucking awesome. You know, like TOTALLY. And I swear to God I've never said that before. I mean I liked your profile and everything but the real thing is just like, FUCK.

GIRL   Really? I mean like you really mean that like for real?

BOY   Ye-ah! You're just like . . . *(makes the gesture of stabbing himself in the heart)* ahhhhh! And your ass? Your ass is like . . . it's like Iron Man's suit. It's like Batman's Batmobile. Your ass is so fucking perfect it's like a piece of ART.

31

Giggles.

And it's not just your ass, it's like everything. Swear to God. And I'm not objectifying you 'cause when I say everything, I really mean like EVERYTHING. Including your personality and shit.

GIRL   Well, I'm glad 'cause I'm just like . . . *(pretends to pounce on him)* Roar! I'm just like this guy is like OH MY GOD and I mean I'm sorry but like I totally want to get into your pants.

BOY   Fuck yeah.

He pounces on her. They go at it again. This time, he tears himself away.

And you know what? You know what? I fucking LOVE the fact that you're GF too. Love it. I mean usually I'm just like the weird guy, you know? The like HIGH MAINTENANCE dude. Like, "What do you mean you can't have a burger? It's ORGANIC."

GIRL   Yeah and like no matter how many times you tell them, they never remember, right? Sometimes I feel like I should have it tattooed on my forehead: GF. GLUTEN-FREE.

BOY   But they still wouldn't get it 'cause they're like morons or something. The other day, the guy at the restaurant was like, "Gluten? Isn't that a muscle in your ASS?"

GIRL   TOTALLY.

Footsteps. They try to act casual. She adjusts her clothes. He examines his shoes. They acknowledge the invisible passerby with a smile or a nod.

BOY   So anyway . . .

She checks the time on her cell.

GIRL   I should probably go.

BOY   Yeah me too.

GIRL   So um . . .

BOY   Well so like do you think— . . . I mean I'm just asking, you know but do you think maybe we can do this again some other night and uh . . . well . . . maybe get to the "get into your pants" part?

GIRL   I was gonna ask you the same thing.

BOY   Cool.

He's happy. Then confused.

So . . . does that mean yes?

GIRL   Yes.

BOY   Sweet!

A victory dance.

GIRL   But I have, I mean I hope you don't mind but I need to ask you something before. I mean before we like, you know . . .

BOY   Sure. Anything. Shoot.

GIRL   And it's not I mean don't take this the wrong way OK 'cause it's really about me. Like I just need to ask you this thing 'cause well . . . 'cause it's like important to me.

BOY   I don't have another girl on the side if that's what you wanna know.

GIRL   Oh no, that's not— . . . I mean that's great. But like I'm cool with that. Not that you SHOULD have another girl but sometimes you gotta check what's in the other store to make sure you're buying the right thing. So like, as long as you tell me 'cause I'm not too good with lying and shit—that just makes me mad and then I get real ugly—but as long as you tell me I'm cool.

BOY   OK. I'm cool too. I mean, you know. You shop, I shop . . . *(pause)* But uh . . . like . . . are you a big shopper?

GIRL   Depends. Right now I'm kind of digging what I see in this store.

BOY   Oh yeah?

He struts.

Good merchandise, huh? Slick. Fully equipped. *(to someone across the street)* Hey! Don't you agree that this here is some good merchandise?

She hits him playfully.

GIRL   Stop!

He gets an appreciative whistle in response.

BOY   See? But the thing is you really gotta take it for a test drive if you wanna feel the HORSEPOWER.

GIRL   I AM gonna take it for a test drive. But first—

She takes out her cell.

Promise you won't get mad?

BOY   Promise.

She turns her back to him and texts something. After a beat, his cell shouts or barks—something obnoxious. He checks it. She looks at him expectantly.

GIRL   So?

BOY   What the fuck?

GIRL   Hey, you promised.

BOY   Are you serious?

GIRL   Well yeah.

BOY   You're asking me this?

GIRL   Yeah.

BOY   Like, you're REALLY asking me this?

GIRL   Yeah. I'm really asking you this.

BOY   You don't know me. You don't know my life. Why are you asking me this?

GIRL   'Cause.

BOY   'Cause why?

GIRL	'Cause if we gonna do this, we should do it right.
BOY	This is not doing it right. This is getting into a guy's BUSINESS. And I don't like people getting into my business. Don't like it one bit.
GIRL	Come on. It's not that big of a deal.
BOY	It IS that big of a deal! It's like a HUGE fucking deal, OK? I mean I don't ask you to like— . . . I don't know but like I don't make ASSUMPTIONS about you.
GIRL	I'm not making— . . . Look, if you want me to ride your HORSEPOWER, the least you can do is put a little effort into it. I mean HELLO-O? I don't know what kind of girls you've been hanging with but I got STANDARDS.
BOY	Well, actually—
GIRL	And sorry if that's like annoying to you but that's just the way it is.

Her cell sings.

	That's my dad. *(She picks up.)* Hi, Dad . . . Yeah, I know. I'm almost there. I'll be home in like fifteen minutes, OK? . . . OK. Bye.
BOY	Look, I'm clean, OK? I'm VERY clean. I'm like cleaner than fucking Mr. Clean.
GIRL	You don't know that.
BOY	I DO know that.
GIRL	No, you don't. Nobody knows. You can't know unless you get tested.
BOY	Maybe you got the tightest hardest most like unbelievably awesome ass in the whole fucking world and maybe I'm just like dying to lick every inch of it like the frosting off a doughnut but I'm not—you hear me?—NOT getting tested. And I can't believe you even asked. That's just like . . . RUDE!

GIRL	Chill, OK? So I asked you to get tested. What? You can't do that for your girl?
BOY	Why, 'cause you think I'm just like Mr. Irresponsible? Mr. Testosterone-brain? Mr. like I just think about myself and FUCK THE WORLD?
GIRL	I told you, it's not about YOU.
BOY	Well it sure FEELS like it.
GIRL	It's about ME. 'Cause it took me like TWO YEARS to clean myself up so I don't wanna be with some guy who's gonna MESS ME UP again. I mean, you know? You're probably fine—
BOY	I AM fine!
GIRL	—but if you're not . . . well, I don't know but like it doesn't mean that it's your fault or anything. I mean that's how it happened for me. I was just talking with that girl at school, you know Briana, the one with the big boobs. She's always busting my balls and she was like, Girl . . . just looking at you I can tell your numbers are OFF THE CHART. And I was like, SHUT UP. 'Cause she didn't know, you know? And you can't tell just by LOOKING at someone.
BOY	EXACTLY.
GIRL	But she was like, I'M TELLING YOU and she was pissing me off 'cause she's always like Miss Perfect and everything so I went and got tested just to shut her up. So like the woman at the clinic asked me all these questions and I was doing real well but then she said to me, she said, Girl, you got a PROBLEM. And I was like, NO I DON'T. 'Cause I had already made my dad trade his SUV for a hybrid and change all the light bulbs in the house so I KNEW I was OK. But she was like, I got your numbers right here in front of me and they say you got a carbon footprint the size of TEXAS. And I was like, EXCUSE ME? And she was like, Uh-huuuuuuh. And I was like, "Are you calling me a POLLUTER?" 'Cause maybe

I've never been to Texas but I know it's BIG so I get your metaphor, LADY. And I was so fucking insulted, I was like, You know what? Fuck this shit. Fuck you, fuck Briana, and fuck everything! 'Cause like WHATEVER. I mean, it's not like I was still using PLASTIC BAGS! But then a few weeks later, I went to this place where I used to go with my dad. It's way up north, you know, like WAY THE FUCK. And there's like NOTHING up there, like for real, just mountains and forests and lakes, nothing else. So we're there, right, and except for the mosquitoes, it's like AWESOME and my uncle comes for a visit 'cause he always comes for a visit, it's like a tradition. And my uncle is this SUPER COOL guy, you know like he SNOWBOARDS and he's been around the world and stuff so he's like AMAZING. And so he has this small plane and he used to fly us around, one by one 'cause it's a two-seater so you can only have one passenger. And I used to go with him a lot and throw up all the time 'cause on top of being GF I got real bad motion sickness but I didn't care I would go anyway 'cause from up there, you can see really far and it's like this GIANT green carpet for like FOREVER, you know? For like AS FAR AS YOU CAN SEE ... And I know it freaks people out sometimes to see big nature like that but me, it makes me feel SAFE. 'Cause I look at those trees and I tell myself, I tell myself as long as there's more of them than of us, nothing can go wrong, you know? And so like, my uncle asks me if I want to go flying again and of course I say yes and we go and I throw up for old times' sake and it's like FUCKING AWESOME all over again with the forests and the mountains and the blue lakes but then we get to one of my favourite spots you know and ... and ... *(She tears up.)* Fuck.

He makes a move toward her. She waves him off.

I'm fine ... *(She breathes.)* So anyway, I'm on the plane and I look down and ... and you know all those mountains? . . . They were BALD . . . Just like . . . Nothing. Gone. All the trees had been cut. And it was like . . . it was like looking at a cancer patient who's just lost all her hair . . . It was so PAINFUL . . . 'Cause you know in your guts that it's WRONG. Nobody has to tell you. You just KNOW. And so I was looking at these BALD mountains with only the stumps left all over like ugly SCARS and I thought . . . I thought about the clinic and it finally clicked, you know, I thought . . . It's ME. I'm that mountain's CANCER . . .

A beat.

BOY   Here.

He offers his sleeve. She wipes her eyes and nose with it.

GIRL   Great. Now you're gonna think I'm all girlie and shit.

BOY   Girlie's cool. I got no problems with girlie.

GIRL   Whatever.

BOY   Aw, come on. Girlie's better than a CANCER.

GIRL   Don't make fun.

BOY   I'm not!

GIRL   So anyway . . . After that, I . . . I decided to DO something, you know . . . To make it better for the EARTH. So my dad and I, we stopped using the dryer and started hanging the laundry instead. And me and another girl—that was MY idea—we walk my sister and her classmates to school. That way the parents don't have to drive them. And the next thing I wanna do is get a compost bin—

BOY   I can help you with that.

GIRL   You can?

BOY   I built the one at our place.

GIRL   You got a COMPOST BIN?

BOY   My mom's an energy auditor. We got everything.

GIRL	Oh.

A beat. He cups his ear as if he's just heard something.

BOY	Did I just hear a thump?
GIRL	What?
BOY	Was that a thump? Did you just like fall off a really HIGH horse?
GIRL	Fuck off.
BOY	'Cause I mean, I couldn't hear very clearly but that's kind of what it sounded like.
GIRL	OK, so I feel like an HUGE FUCKING ASSHOLE, are you happy? I mean, how the fuck was I supposed to know your mom is an ENERGY AUDITOR?

She turns to leave.

BOY	Whoa, whoa, wait a minute . . .
GIRL	What.

He types something on his phone.

BOY	Where's that clinic at?
GIRL	Why?
BOY	I wanna know.

The GIRL's phone sighs seductively.

GIRL	Did you just text me?

She checks her cell. Reads the message.

	Shut up.
BOY	It's true.
GIRL	You're just fucking with me.
BOY	No, I swear to God, it's true.
GIRL	What, like you really mean this?
BOY	Yeah. And I'm gonna get tested just to prove it to you. But you better watch out 'cause my carbon

footprint is gonna kick your carbon footprint's ASS.

GIRL   Ha! Good luck. 'Cause in case you didn't know, I got MAJORLY AWESOME numbers.

BOY   Then I'm gonna have even MORE majorly awesome numbers.

GIRL   Dude, my numbers are so awesome, I'm almost in the SINGLE DIGITS.

BOY   Girl, I live with the energy efficiency QUEEN. You got any idea what that means? That means I'm gonna have NEGATIVE numbers. I'm gonna be so fucking energy efficient that my sole EXISTENCE is gonna reduce carbon emissions.

A beat.

GIRL   OK, that's kind of hot.

BOY   Oh yeah? Like your climate is warming?

GIRL   Maybe like a degree or two.

She moves toward him seductively. He jumps back just before she touches him.

BOY   Then see you tomorrow. AFTER I get tested.

He takes off. A beat. Her phone sighs. She checks it. A big grin.

GIRL   Fucker.

Blackout.

Sisters
An homage to Chekhov
by Per Brask

Sisters is an adaptation of Chekhov's *Three Sisters*. On Irena's twentieth birthday, she, Olga, and, Masha fight provincial boredom by discussing the best way to live—by work, thrilling romances, or self-sacrificing love. If only they could go to Moscow their dreams would be fulfilled. In the meantime, an attempt to remember the poem by Pushkin must suffice.

CHARACTER LIST

Olga
Masha
Irena

...

Per Brask has taught at the University of Winnipeg since 1982. He has published poetry, short stories, plays, translation, interviews, and essays in a number of journals and books. He has written three other Chekhov adaptations in addition to the one published here.

Sisters

OLGA, MASHA, and IRENA sit in large armchairs some distance apart from each other. OLGA, dressed in blue, is marking student essays; MASHA, dressed in black, is reading Samuel Johnson; and IRENA, dressed in white, is daydreaming. In the background someone is playing the cello very softly. A rear projection of a mansion.

OLGA   I'm twenty-eight.

IRENA   I'm twenty—today.

MASHA   I'm twenty-two—married.

OLGA   I would have been fond of my husband.

MASHA   *(laughing)* You're talking nonsense.

IRENA   We must work, work, work. How beautiful it would be to come home exhausted from fixing the roads or plowing snow or teaching school.

OLGA   I get irritated with my pupils and I have this persistent headache.

IRENA   I long for important work. If we lived in Moscow, Olga . . .

| OLGA | To Moscow, as soon as we possibly can. |

IRENA ... I would probably already be at work in some deeply meaningful way and I would find the woman that I dream of every night. Maybe I could become a writer or ... Masha could visit us every summer.

MASHA *(whistles)*

OLGA Stop that, Masha.

MASHA *(gets up and dances a few steps)* A green oak ... A green oak grows on the shore of the bay ... and ... and ... *(She sits down again.)* Oh, what does it matter?

IRENA Pushkin ...

MASHA Don't mind me. I'm depressed.

OLGA I understand you, Masha. Oh, how I understand you.

IRENA I don't know why there's so much joy in my heart. I woke up and I just knew how I ought to live.

OLGA You look pretty today, Masha.

IRENA I know what you're doing, Olga. You think I can't be serious because you still see me as a little girl. I am twenty, you know.

MASHA *(whistles)*

OLGA Please ...

There's a brief pause during which OLGA goes back to marking, MASHA to her reading, and IRENA to her daydreaming. The cello music gets louder during the pause.

MASHA *(suddenly)* Listen! Here at the end of Samuel Johnson's *The History of Rasselas, Prince of Abissinia* we learn in "The Conclusion, in which nothing is concluded" that Rasselas, his sister, and their poet guide all come to different "choices of life" after their long investigation into the various ways humans seek happiness. Rasselas desires a kingdom "in which he might administer justice in his own person." The Princess desires "to learn all the sciences," establish a college for women and "by conversing with the old, and educating the young" to "divide her time between the acquisition and communication of wisdom." Imlac, their poet guide, and the astronomer they befriended on the way are "contented to be driven along the stream of life without directing their course to any particular port." In retrospect, given the long search and their various reactions to their experiences and encounters with people's ideas of proper living, the fact that these characters should come to different conclusions about their choice of life makes complete sense, doesn't it? *(OLGA and IRENA stare at her, saying nothing.)* So this is Johnson's insight, his wisdom made manifest in this story. There is not one way to happiness or proper choice of life and equally there are innumerable ways of going wrong. What all the promising ways of pursuing have in common is that the pursuit must be consistent with the character's nature. It is in this way that I believe the outcome of Johnson's non-conclusion provides a glimpse of wisdom. The choices his characters make are consistent with whom we've learned them to be in the course of the story. So, that's what's at stake, knowing your character, isn't it?

IRENA	*(beat)* I don't think I'd enjoy working at the post office or at city hall, though.
OLGA	I think love is the answer.
MASHA	A green oak grows on the shore of the bay and around that oak / a golden chain . . .
IRENA	/ a golden chain . . . *(MASHA and IRENA chuckle.)*
OLGA	I'm being serious.
MASHA & IRENA	Sorry.
IRENA	Parliamo italiano.
OLGA	Why?

45

IRENA	It's more romantic.
OLGA	I'm not seeking romance. I want love. I want a deep love cultivated over years of a healthy engaging companionship. I just need someone who'll begin the process with me.
IRENA	Dear Olga, how will you ever find an engaging companion here? The theatre is banal and the book clubs are undiscerning. You'll end up marrying some mid-level officer and sent off to Poland or Siberia at a moment's notice. Father died a year ago, let's finally sell the house and move back to Moscow.
OLGA	It's not that simple.
IRENA	Why not?
OLGA	Well, for one thing I'm established here and so is Masha.
IRENA	You just said, "To Moscow, as soon as we possibly can."
OLGA	Yes, as soon as we possibly can.
IRENA	You're scared, you mean.
OLGA	Honestly, yes, I am. Also I don't like the idea of leaving Masha behind.
IRENA	You're not making any sense. She chose to get married to somebody here.
OLGA	Still. Anyway, making sense doesn't come into it. I do want to move to Moscow—at the right time.
IRENA	The right time is now. I don't know how much more I can take of these people. Pretending to be interested in their little lives. It's driving me mad. How am I going to dedicate myself to improving the world around here? I need some competent feedback from other people who aren't my sisters. Who here will discourse on Samuel Johnson out of the blue, but Masha? Moments ago there was joy in my heart. I knew how to live. Now that's *(makes puff sound)* . . .

OLGA & MASHA   Sorry . . .

IRENA   I still think meaning is ultimately found in work.

MASHA   Then go and find some work.

IRENA   I will, too. Work—to transform the material into the cultural.

Again there's a brief pause during which OLGA *goes back to her marking,* MASHA *to her reading, and* IRENA *to her daydreaming. The cello music gets louder during the pause.*

OLGA   *(suddenly)* Another angel flew past. *(beat)* The other day I came across a quote by Benjamin Whichcote, you know, the leader of the Cambridge Platonists, actually stating, "If it were not for Sin, *we* should converse together as *Angels* do." Except I read it as, "If it were not *a* Sin, *we* should converse together as *Angels* do." Which made so much sense to me, understanding sin as mistake, as not on the mark, as missing the mark, because it would indeed be a sin to converse as *Angels* do. Apart from no one knowing how *Angels* do converse, the attempt itself would prevent us from becoming more fully human; aiming at becoming anything but human would give us a false target and that makes me wonder why Whichcote would ever wish for it?

IRENA   *(beat)* "How am I to live?— According to the law of God. What real result will come of my life?— Eternal torment or eternal bliss. What meaning has life that death does not destroy?— Union with the eternal God: heaven." Uhhh. ". . . faith makes it possible to live. Faith still remained to me as irrational as it was before, but I could not but admit that it alone gives mankind a reply to the questions of life, and that consequently it makes life possible." *(*OLGA *and* MASHA *stare at her.)* Tolstoy's confession.

MASHA & OLGA   We know.

IRENA	So through work we can serve humanity. That is my faith and it will sustain me and be my buffer against life's inevitable disappointments.
MASHA	Dearest sisters, there's something I'm burning to tell you ...
OLGA & IRENA	We know.
MASHA	... I'm having an affair with the colonel. I love him.
OLGA & IRENA	Ughhh.
MASHA	He sends me over the moon. I know he's married and has two little girls, but it doesn't seem to matter. I find him magnetic when he talks about life in the future—not that he does anything about it, but then it's not next week he thinks about. It's life in the far distant future. So, I suppose we can't do anything about it anyway. He has this mathematical view of how in each generation there will be more people like us, until eventually, I suppose, we are in the majority and things will be so much better—more cultured. He likes opera.
IRENA	The baron thinks that everything will change but that life itself, individual lives will face the same sorts of problems always. Life follows its own laws, he says. I don't know what to think. He sniffs around me all the time and says that he loves me, but I can't say the same. I can't even say that my feelings don't go in that general direction, because they actually go in both directions. But I couldn't love him back. He's so ugly, though he is quite refined. I suppose I could marry him, but I'd need the woman of my dreams also—and she's in Moscow.
OLGA & MASHA	Moscow ...
IRENA	And to that chain a tomcat is tied ...

OLGA *and* MASHA *look at* IRENA. *They all smile and take this as a cue to get up, hold hands, and dance in a circle.*

ALL	*(with increasing speed)* A green oak grows on the shore of the bay, and around that oak a golden chain, and to that chain a tomcat is tied . . . A green oak grows on the shore of the bay, and around that oak a golden chain, and to that chain a tomcat is tied . . . A green oak grows on the shore of the bay, and around that oak a golden chain, and to that chain a tomcat is tied . . . A green oak grows on the shore of the bay, and around that oak a golden chain, and to that chain a tomcat is tied . . . *(They stop and look at each other, chuckling.)*
OLGA	Why can't we remember the rest?
MASHA	It'll come back. It's been a long time. What does it matter?
IRENA	The other day I couldn't remember the Italian for ceiling. I feel as though my brain has shrivelled up. I'm only twenty but I've gotten thinner and uglier. Time is passing and there's no satisfaction in sight. I'm sinking into some kind of abyss. And I felt so happy this morning. Determined. I had hope, but it's not even lunchtime and that hope for a genuine, refined life seems very distant now.

They all sit. There's another brief pause during which OLGA *goes back to her marking,* MASHA *to her reading, and* IRENA *to her daydreaming. The cello music gets louder during the pause.*

MASHA	You have to grab your happiness in little bits and be fine with that. You may grow hard and irritable and withdrawn like I am most of the time. But when the tingling starts you just go for it.
IRENA	Day and night he circles the tree.
OLGA	When he runs clockwise he sings a song.
MASHA	Counter-clockwise he tells a tale.

The sisters chuckle, MASHA *then whistles.*

OLGA	That is such an uncouth habit, Masha.
MASHA	I know, but what does it matter?
OLGA	It feels like chalk on slate.

MASHA	*(whistles)*
IRENA	That's not funny, Masha!
MASHA	Sorry. I couldn't help it.
IRENA	The truth is that our dear brother has become shallow since Father died. He says he feels released from all that education. Well, what's occupying him instead is gambling. He's built up huge debts and now he's mortgaged the house to the hilt. And his wife is having an affair with his boss.
OLGA & MASHA	We know.
IRENA	It could make me scream. *(about to do so)*
OLGA & MASHA	Well, don't.
IRENA	Fine.

Beat.

OLGA	Wasn't it Arthur Schopenhauer who said something to the effect that as long as we are wilful, that as long as we are filled with wants we will be preoccupied by hope and fear and we will never achieve true happiness or calm. As long as we focus on evermore persistent wants we are tied to Ixion's flaming wheel of cravings.
MASHA	How very Buddhist of him.
IRENA	He also said that it is as impossible to teach someone to be virtuous as it is to teach someone how to be a genius and that it is as silly to expect that our systems of morality should produce noble people, as it is to expect philosophy of art to inspire artists. *(beat)* So what's the point? How do we get to do the kind of nothing that will ease our suffering? Life for us, we three sisters, has not been easy. Other people would think that it has been, that it's been beautiful. But the truth is that we've been stifled, like weeds in a garden. Why this constant suffering?
OLGA	If only we knew. If only we knew.

IRENA   I guess if that's how God wills it, then we must soldier on, find our way. *(looking toward the heavens)* But a little direction would be nice.

OLGA   If only we knew. If only we knew.

MASHA   What does it matter? I can barely remember Mother's face. Undoubtedly people will forget about us. We'll all be forgotten. Well, enough of that. *(She gets up and holds her hands out to her sisters.)* One more time!

ALL   *(dancing in a circle)* A green oak grows on the shore of the bay, and around that oak a golden chain, and to that chain a tomcat is tied. Day and night he circles the tree: When he runs clockwise he sings a song and counter-clockwise he tells a tale . . . A green oak grows on the shore of the bay, and around that oak a golden chain, and to that chain a tomcat is tied. Day and night he circles the tree: When he runs clockwise he sings a song and counter-clockwise he tells a tale . . . A green oak grows on the shore of the bay, and around that oak a golden chain, and to that chain a tomcat is tied. Day and night he circles the tree: When he runs clockwise he sings a song and counter-clockwise he tells a tale . . . A green oak grows on the shore of the bay, and around that oak a golden chain, and to that chain a tomcat is tied. Day and night he circles . . .

OLGA   *(letting go)* Enough, enough! I'm dizzy.

They all fall into their chairs, chuckling. There's another brief pause during which OLGA goes back to her marking, MASHA to her reading, and IRENA to her daydreaming. The cello music gets louder during the pause. A gong sounds offstage.

      Lunchtime. There will be meat pie in honour of your birthday, Irena.

IRENA   Do I really have to go in there with all those people?

MASHA	*(playfully pulling* IRENA *out of her chair)* Yes, you do. But I don't. I'll come later on. I'm too depressed now to be good company.
IRENA	No, no, please stay.
OLGA	Now you two, enough of that. Get going.
IRENA & MASHA	Yes, yes, yes. *(They wander off arm in arm.)*
OLGA	*(Picks up her students' essays and* MASHA's *book. Looks out.)* If only we knew. *(She exits. The cello fades as do the lights.)*

THE END

Cook
by David James Brock

The private cook for a demanding family interviews a boy who wishes to become the family's next meal.

Cook was first produced by Theatre Lab at Toronto's Campbell House Museum in October 2013 as part of the site-specific show *You Can Sleep When You're Dead*. It was directed by Michael Orlando with the following cast:

Cook	EricaOverholt
Meat	Colin Edwards
Butcher	Daniel de Pass
A lot of bodies	The cast, crew and friends of Theatre Lab

CHARACTER LIST
Cook
Meat
Butcher
A lot of bodies

SETTING
A kitchen

A NOTE ON THE TEXT
/   overlapping dialogue
. . .   a sound, not speech, but conveys meaning.

...

David James Brock is a playwright, poet, and librettist whose plays and operas have been performed in cities across Canada, the US, and the UK. His play *Wet* won the 2011 Herman Voaden National Playwriting Competition, and he is also the author of the collection of poetry *Everyone is CO_2*. David is co-creator of *Breath Cycle*, an opera for singers with cystic fibrosis, which was nominated for a 2014 Royal Philharmonic Society Award. Learn more about his work at www.davidjamesbrock.com.

Cook

And in the other room, Mary Maloney began to giggle.
                    —Roald Dahl, *Lamb to the Slaughter*

Kitchen. Bodies everywhere (audience included). Some move slightly. Some are still.

Hot soup in the fireplace. COOK *chops onions.*

COOK   *(Sings. Finds her own tune.)*
                    I love you in the guts—   [BODIES
                                                      Lummmmm . . . .]

                    a glutton for you, I am nuts for
                    you, my little lamb.   [BODIES
                                                      Hummmmm . . . .]

                    Stuff me in your arms—   [BODIES
                                                      Mmmm . . . .]
                    your charms upon my body, dear.
                    Our feast, it will be grand.   [BODIES
                                                      Ummmm . . . .]

BUTCHER enters. MEAT *walks just behind.*

BUTCHER   Smells great, lady.

MEAT   This is wonderful.

BUTCHER   Shut the fuck up!

BODIES   / Shhhhhh!

55

COOK	Something missing. Always something missing.

MEAT tastes the soup.

MEAT	Thumb.
COOK	You think so?

BUTCHER tastes the soup.

BUTCHER	Ah, definitely thumb.
MEAT	Take mine.
COOK	Whoa, hold on now. Doesn't work that way.
MEAT	It's a fine and tender thumb. Not hardened by a life of manual labour.
COOK	/ Anyone have a thumb?

One or more of the BODIES raises a hand, or specifically, a thumb. COOK goes to one of the bodies, lops its thumb off, tosses it in the soup.

MEAT	It would be my honour to serve The Family.
COOK	Chatty. Won't make for a fine and tender tongue.

COOK inspects MEAT.

	Where'd you find this one?
BUTCHER	He's my brother's boy.
COOK	And your brother doesn't object?
BUTCHER	My brother was The Family's Christmas dinner, love.
COOK	Ah yes. *Him.* Where's my brain?
MEAT	My brain will make great appetizer. Cold, on parsnip purée. With basic seasoning.
	I'd think . . . thyme.

COOK slaps him.

COOK	Shut the fuck up!
BODIES	/ Shhhhhh!
MEAT	Yes ma'am.

COOK slaps him again.

COOK   I said—

BODIES   / Shhhhhh!

Silence. Examining MEAT.

COOK   Your father was tasty.

The Family raved about it for a week.

Tasty ancestry is a definite plus. Meat tastes like its parents' meat.

And he went willingly, which kept the meat from going tough.

You can taste fear.

We did him with lemon potatoes, right?

BUTCHER   That's the one.

COOK   You'd go willingly, would you? Don't want to serve The Family struggled meat.

MEAT nods.

What's your chemistry?

BUTCHER   Go 'head, boy.

MEAT   Never alcohol. Never sugar. My flesh is not poison. My meat will not poison The Family. Pinch me.

BUTCHER   Pinch him.

MEAT   Pinch me.

COOK pricks him instead. Tastes his blood.

COOK   Hm.

BUTCHER   Hm?

COOK   Yes. Hm.

MEAT   Good, yes?

COOK   *(to BUTCHER)* Leave us.

BUTCHER   Yep.

> *To* MEAT. *Shaking hands.*
>
> Good luck.

MEAT   You promise . . . when it's time . . . you'll try me, Uncle.

BUTCHER   If it's my destiny . . . yeah. All right. I'll eat you, boy.

> BUTCHER *leaves.*

COOK   Sit.

> MEAT *sits while* COOK *casually stirs.*
>
> We don't take people against their will, you know. We aren't kidnappers.
>
> Are we?!

BODIES   Noooooo!

COOK   So why?

MEAT   Why?

BODIES   / Whyyyyyyy?

COOK   YES! I SAID "WHY?"

> *Silence.*

MEAT   We are poor.

COOK   Everyone is poor. The world is poor.

MEAT   The Family is not poor.

COOK   No. The Family is not poor.

MEAT   We were poor before my father left to be in your service.

COOK   We, huh?

MEAT   My mother, my sisters, and my younger brother—who will someday, also make good meat—we eat what we can find.

It is my job to prepare our meals. To hide what our meat originally was . . . Through preparation.

	My younger siblings believe that the mice I cook is veal.
COOK	Why?
MEAT	Because I tell them it is veal.
	After my father came to you . . . and you served him to The Family . . .
COOK	/ With lemon potatoes.
MEAT	With lemon potatoes.
	Then we had a little bit of money.
	When we had money, we spent it on real food.
	It was the only time in my life I've eaten chicken, beef, pork. I would cook it for *my* family.
	It was the happiest *my* family ever was.
	We could finally use the teeth in our mouths instead of simply putting food in our mouth, wetting the food, swirling it around with our tongue . . . then swallowing.
	Pretending to chew and taste. We finally chewed and tasted.
	We spent all the money The Family paid us for my father's meat. We were full.
	And then there was no more meat. And then we were not quite as happy.
	One month after my father left, we were once again just another poor family. Meatless.
	Hungry.
COOK	Eating mice.
MEAT	Eating veal.
	When the cats could catch it.
	Then, eating the cats.
	I would like to give my mother, my sisters, and my younger brother another happy month like that . . . being full.

COOK	And then after that month?
MEAT	I suppose they'll have to come up with a solution.
COOK	Your brother?
MEAT	If he chooses this . . .
COOK	Torturous life.
MEAT	You would turn down a meal just because it can't make you full forever?
COOK	Knowing the difference, I might.
MEAT	Life for us is month to month.
COOK	/ A torturous life this poverty business, isn't it?
MEAT	But a month is a month.

Pause.

My legs and arms will be best grilled. My eyes boiled.

Stew my heart with shallots and a red wine broth.

COOK	You've done this . . .
MEAT	I'm a great cook, ma'am.
COOK	Hm.
MEAT	/ Works with the mice anyway.
COOK	Human meat is not mouse meat.
MEAT	/ Though no, we've never eaten—
COOK	A different mode of preparation all together.
MEAT	Man.
COOK	/ A great cook who is always hungry.

Pause.

MEAT	I am a tragic figure.

Pause.

Was my father really delicious?

COOK	The Family still raves about it.

	In fact, I have a hard time living him down.
	"Not as good as last Christmas," they said after Easter.
MEAT	Ah.
COOK	"Not as good as Christmas."
MEAT	Hm.
COOK	"NOT AS GOOD AS CHRISTMAS!"
BODIES	/ Whyyyyyyy?

Pause.

COOK	Nah. I won't accept you.
MEAT	Why not?
COOK	I don't want The Family to ever have it so good again.
MEAT	You'd serve The Family inferior meat?
COOK	That they ever knew the difference was my great mistake.
MEAT	Please!
COOK	No no no . . . They must forget your father's meat.
MEAT	We're desperate!
COOK	You'll be delicious, I have no doubt.
MEAT	I am desperate.
COOK	We are all desperate! Aren't we?
BODIES	YES!
COOK	You are desperate to get a job. I am desperate to keep mine.
MEAT	You need me!
COOK	Sure, I can cook your father, then you, then your brother, your sisters . . . then what?
	When your family's out, The Family will once again wonder and wonder and WONDER!
	You are too short-sighted.

61

MEAT   Then what?

*COOK examines a body intimately, distracting herself, thinking
. . . thinking . . . think—*

COOK   A system.

MEAT   . . .

Thinking.

COOK   That.

COOK points at MEAT's groin.

MEAT   There's hardly any meat there!

COOK   I don't mean cook it.

MEAT   I don't understand.

COOK   Babies.

MEAT   You don't mean . . . eat babies?

COOK   Your brain is tender, isn't it?

MEAT   . . .

COOK   Make them! Reproduce.

Farm your babies.

Feed them. Fatten them.

When they grow large enough, I will use *their*
meat. You can supply this kitchen for years to
come.

Your brother's and sisters' litters too. Get *them*
breeding.

Maybe even that butcher uncle of yours, I'll have
to taste him. Farmers.

For that, yeah . . . I will pay you. Your family will
grow rich.

You will have all the beef, chicken . . . ever eaten
a fish?

MEAT   No.

COOK   You will grow fat on it.

You will chew and breed and taste and breed. You will need a title of course.

Thinking, thinking, think—

Office of Special Occasions.

Yes. *Your* family will be *The* Family's private farmers under the Office of Special Occasions. And you will be . . . Officer.

MEAT   You can arrange this?

COOK   If you can you arrange . . .

MEAT   . . .

COOK   The baby part.

MEAT   Oh. That. Yeah. I think I can do that.

COOK   Have you?

MEAT   Have I what?

COOK   If you're asking, you haven't . . .

MEAT   Haven't what?

COOK   Sexed up a lady body.

MEAT   Oh. No.

COOK   You were willing to become meat before you . . .

BODIES laugh, hoot, holler.

You really are veal aren't you?

BODIES   Veal! Veal! Veal!

COOK   Well, let's go then.

COOK clears some chopped onions from the table.

MEAT   Go?

COOK   Let's see if you're a breeder . . .

MEAT   Here?

COOK   Trust me, the bedrooms of this house are no better.

MEAT	But the onions.
COOK	What better place for it than on a bed of onions?
MEAT	My first time.

Pause.

COOK	I'm waiting, Officer.
MEAT	I accept your proposal.
COOK	Of course you do.
	Now cook.

MEAT and COOK begin breeding future meat on a bed of chopped onions. BODIES rise and hum the same song from the beginning.

One BODY stirs the soup, maybe popping off her own thumb and dropping it in.

The rest of the bodies surround MEAT and COOK, effectively becoming a final curtain . . .

THE END

The Auction
by Trina Davies

Kate has had enough. Ernie has brought enough auction junk home to fill a caboose in the west pasture. She throws his latest purchase at him and locks him out of the house. As he figures out a way to get back inside to the waiting dinner, they both discover that they've been avoiding something for way too long.

The Auction premiered at the Globe Theatre in Regina, Saskatchewan, directed by Angus Ferguson. It is also a scene in the full-length *West of the Third Meridian*.

CHARACTER LIST

Kate   late thirties
Ernie   early forties

SETTING

A 1940s farmhouse

...

Trina Davies is a playwright based in Vancouver, BC. Trina's award-winning plays include *Shatter*, *Multi User Dungeon*, *The Auction*, and *Waxworks*. Her play *The Romeo Initiative* won her the Enbridge playRites Award for Established Artist in 2008 and was a finalist for the Governor General's Literary Award for Drama in 2012. Her plays have been performed across Canada and in a number of other countries including the United States, Germany, Italy, and India. Her work has been translated into Italian and German. She has participated in artist residencies at the Stratford Festival in Ontario and the Banff Centre for Arts and Creativity. She is currently working on a play entitled *The Bone Bridge* (winner of the 2014 Uprising National Playwriting Competition for plays concerning social justice) and a commission from Theatre Calgary for *Silence: Mabel and Alexander Graham Bell*. Trina is a member of the Alberta Playwrights' Network, the Playwrights Theatre Centre, and the Playwrights Guild of Canada.

The Auction

Lights come up on the kitchen of a late 1940s prairie farmhouse. Around the sides of the room there are kitchen appliances and cupboards. In the centre of the room is a small kitchen table that is set for dinner. There is also a sizable wooden crate (apple box) on the table. There is a telephone in the room. There is a window that slides open in the upstage wall. There is also a large screen door that is latched shut.

As the lights come up, KATE *is standing near the table beside the wooden crate. She takes a plate from the crate and throws it against the wall near the screen door. She pauses for a moment, then sits at the table and composes herself. It is quiet and there is a long pause.*

ERNIE appears in the screen door. He is in a tuxedo that is much too small for him. He has been drinking.

ERNIE   Let me explain /

KATE gets up again and throws another piece of china near the door. ERNIE *disappears from view.*

After a moment, ERNIE *appears again, this time just pressing his face against the screen door as he hides his body around the corner.*

Katie?

KATE   What am I supposed to do with chipped dishes?

ERNIE   But the man said they're real bone china. I thought you'd like them.

        They're from England or someplace. Really. Look at the back.

KATE takes a plate in hand and turns it over. As she does so she drops it to the floor.

KATE   Oh, yes. Would you look at that? It does say they're from England.

ERNIE   Katie, come on, let me come back in, will you? That dinner smells good.

KATE   You're two hours late. You're two hours late and you waltz in here with beer on your breath and a crate full of chipped dishes.

ERNIE   Aw, c'mon. They're not all chipped, honey. Take a look.

KATE   Ernie, I don't need any more dishes! And you promised!

ERNIE   Only ten cents. You can't pass up something like that, it'd be a crime!

KATE   And how much for that getup? *(She indicates his tuxedo.)*

ERNIE   Not too much. I got a whole bunch of them! It was a great deal. I got enough for the whole town. Bill's got his on too, we figure we're going get everybody in town dressed up and head down to the hotel for few drinks on Saturday /

KATE   And how much for the beer you drank on the way home?

ERNIE   Aw, Katie, c'mon. We were celebrating, not every day you get your first tuxedo. *(pause)* So, can I come back in?

KATE sits at the table wearily.

KATE	Ernie, do you know how many chamber pots we own?
ERNIE	I haven't counted /
KATE	Forty-three. What are you going to do with forty-three chamber pots?
ERNIE	Sweetie, they were only a penny each.
KATE	And washboards? How many of those?
ERNIE	I don't know. All right, I don't know.
KATE	Eighteen. And do you know how old I was when I married you, Ernie Grey?
ERNIE	Why of course I do, sweetheart. *(pause)* You were . . . You were . . .
KATE	Eighteen. Eighteen years old and I came out West to have an adventure. My mother came to see me off, and she grabbed my arm and said, "Don't go. Don't go, Katie, I'll never see you again." She was afraid it was terribly uncivilized, and that I'd end up married to a dirt farmer.
ERNIE	Well, now that's not fair, I've done the best I could /
KATE	I was a real career girl. And I was pretty too. All the men in town came sniffing around the new girl. Asked me out for dinner, brought flowers to the door of the rooming house. They'd be careful to wear shiny shoes and slicked-back hair—even the farm boys. Did you know that, Ernie? Even the farm boys did that for me.
ERNIE	Katie, let me in and we can talk about this.

KATE gets up and goes to the screen door, ERNIE backs away.

KATE	And you know what else? They had wonderful manners, Ernie. They'd say, "You look lovely tonight, Miss Schmidt," and they'd open all of the doors for me, and pull the chair out at dinner,

and help me on with my overcoat before we went back to the rooming house.

ERNIE   Katie, give me the crate and I'll get rid of the dishes. I promise.

KATE   And then we'd stand on the porch and say good night. Miss Howard at the rooming house would always watch through the lace curtains, even though she said she never did. *(She goes to sweep up the broken dishes.)* And the boy would be nervous, and sometimes his voice would shake a little when he asked me if he could have a kiss good night. I said yes to the dapper ones. When he leaned close to me I could smell this clean-soap smell, like he'd just scoured every part of his body before he came to meet me. And then he'd lean a little closer. Sometimes he'd take my hand, and his palm would be sweaty. He'd lean in and kiss me on the cheek, or if he were daring, he'd lean right in and kiss me on the lips. *(She holds up the dustpan with broken china pieces.)* Can you imagine, Ernie? Can you imagine how many boys kissed me on the lips?

ERNIE   That's not nice talk, Kate. I know I'm late. I know I'm a bad husband. All right, I know it.

Pause.

Can I please come in, Katie. I love you. *(pause)* And I'm hungry.

KATE   The food is on the table.

KATE crosses to the garbage to empty the dustpan and then wanders back to the table. ERNIE eagerly tries the door. It is latched shut and won't open.

ERNIE   What do you want? Do you want me to say I'm sorry. I'm sorry, all right. I'm really, really sorry!

KATE   For what?

ERNIE   For bringing home chipped dishes. I don't know.

KATE   No, I don't think you do know.

ERNIE   I'm really starving. If I can't come in, could you push some food out here?

KATE grabs a bun off of the table. She opens the window and throws it outside, then shuts the window again.

Thanks. *(pause)* Kate, if you really hate the dishes, I'll take them out to the caboose.

KATE   Oh yes, let's put everything in the caboose! Why don't we just go live in the caboose! There are enough chamber pots out there to last us the rest of our lifetime!

ERNIE   Don't start on me about the caboose. It's a solution, isn't it?

KATE   That's right. You go and buy a caboose from the railway and put it out in the west pasture. That fixes everything!

ERNIE   You didn't like all the stuff around the house, always on my case, '"Find a place for this junk, Ernie, I won't have it in my clean house anymore, Ernie."

KATE   *(pause)* Do you know how they talk about you in town? It's a big joke. If there's a chamber pot at auction, they all say "Where's Ernie Grey, he'll buy that." You're the chamber pot man, the junk man, the man who will buy anything.

ERNIE   I don't care what they say. And they don't mean it that way anyway, Katie, you're taking it wrong.

KATE   The man who goes out drinking after every auction to celebrate his new junk.

ERNIE   A man has to have his hobbies, Kate.

KATE   What hobbies do I have, Ernie? Is taking care of your house a hobby? Is cooking your food a hobby? Is waiting around for you to come home drunk with a roll of old hotel carpet underneath your arm a hobby?

Pause.

ERNIE	I'm sorry, Katie, I know that it's been hard. *(pause)* You know what those dishes reminded me of? The first time we went out for dinner at that fancy restaurant. They had all those nice dishes and glasses, and I thought "Whoa boy, I'm out of my league here."
KATE	You kept puffing away on that stinky old pipe you stole from your father.
ERNIE	I thought I looked sophisticated. You looked like a girl who would like sophisticated.
KATE	I suppose I did.
ERNIE	I made you laugh that night.
KATE	*(smiling)* You asked the waiter what part of the duck was the "julienne"?
ERNIE	Well, it said '"julienne of duck." I wasn't going to eat the back end of a duck or something, just because they gave it a fancy name. *(KATE turns to look at him.)* I couldn't even talk all through dinner. Kept thinking I'd do something stupid. And you were so delicate and you even looked sophisticated holding the spoon in your hand. You looked like one of those girls in the advertisements, and you knew what to do with all those glasses and forks and such. You made lively conversation, and all I could do is stammer, say things like, "This is a nice place," and "How about that weather?"
KATE	I think I had to talk for the both of us that night.
ERNIE	And then we got back to Miss Howard's rooming house. I guess I did everything wrong, didn't I? I didn't smell like soap. I smelled like my dad's pipe. And I never asked you if I could kiss you, I just did. You looked pretty surprised.
KATE	You just took my face in your hands and planted a big kiss on me. I think Miss Howard fainted behind the lace curtains!
ERNIE	I'm sorry, Kate. I'm a buffoon.

KATE	Don't you be sorry for that. Do you remember what you said to me?
ERNIE	Yeah. I said "You take my breath away."
KATE	That's all you ever had to say Ernie. That's all you ever had to say.

Pause.

ERNIE	Too bad I didn't have this tuxedo back then, eh?
KATE	I don't think it would have helped, Ernie.
ERNIE	Kate, is that why you married me?
KATE	What do you mean?
ERNIE	Because I said that. Is that why you said yes?
KATE	No, not just that. *(pause)* I haven't made much of a farm wife, have I?
ERNIE	No, you've been great! You just had to . . . well, you had to learn a few things.

The phone rings, KATE *answers.*

KATE	Hello? Hello, Mrs. Eley. Yes. No. Everything is fine. Oh did he? No, no problems here. Yes, well, you see, he won this award, so he needed to get dressed up in a tuxedo. Don't you worry about us, Mrs. Eley. If there's any trouble I'm sure you'll be the first to know. Yes, thank you for your concern, as always. Goodbye now.

KATE *hangs up the phone. She picks up some of the china from the crate and moves over to the window and opens it. She throws the china out of the window while shouting.*

Here, you old bat! Is this what you wanted to see? Look at this! She's finally cracked up! The whole neighbourhood will be relieved that it's finally happened! Be sure to get everyone on the party line, because this is the best news this year! You won't believe what's happening over at the Grey's!

KATE walks away and leaves the window open. ERNIE goes over to the open window and sticks his head through it.

ERNIE   You shouldn't give them anything to talk about.

KATE   *I* shouldn't! Mr. Eley just happened to be going by in his new car and saw "Ernie outside of your house in what looked to be a tuxedo, and there was something flying around and breaking that sounded like glass." She "just wanted to phone to make sure we were all right over here, and that there weren't any hooligans giving us trouble." If they want to talk, then talk!

ERNIE   Kate, it's okay. So she's a busybody, everybody knows that.

KATE   Ernie, she doesn't have a husband walking around in a tuxedo with his arms full of junk.

ERNIE   She's not throwing dishes at her husband, either. This is ridiculous. Let me inside and she won't have anything to see.

ERNIE starts to climb in the window.

KATE   Don't you dare. She'll be on the party line now, telling everyone who will listen. The whole town will be gossiping about us before the sun sets.

ERNIE   Let them talk. I don't care.

KATE   You don't have to face them. You don't have to go to town and look into their pitying eyes and they tilt their heads to the side and they say, "Are you doing all right, dear?" Fine! Fine! I'm fine!

KATE throws a piece of food out of the window. ERNIE ducks and goes to collect the food. He then returns to the window, eating it.

ERNIE   They don't know what to say, Kate.

KATE   It's not fair, Ernie. I loved him more than anything. I don't know what happened. He was beautiful and smart and healthy. He had those bright blue eyes and the rosy red cheeks. He was a smart little boy.

ERNIE	I know.
KATE	I didn't mean to—he just got sick. I don't know why he got sick.
ERNIE	Nobody does, Kate.
KATE	I was standing right here in this kitchen and he pulled himself up on that chair and took a couple of steps right over to me. His little hands were waving all over the place and his chubby face was turned up looking into mine. "What a smart boy you are!" I said. And then a couple of days later . . .
ERNIE	We don't need to talk about this anymore, Kate.
KATE	I'm starting to forget, Ernie. I'm starting to forget him. *(She looks over to* ERNIE, *he avoids her eyes.)* It's not fair. Evelyn Church has seven children. Seven! I go for years with nothing.
ERNIE	You're a good woman, Kate.
KATE	Am I, Ernie? Am I really? Can't have any children, and when I finally do, I can't keep him alive.
ERNIE	Kate, it's done. It's been done for a long time.
KATE	You never! You never said anything except "It'll be okay, Kate," and then you went and bought a caboose.

Pause.

ERNIE	What did you want me to do.
KATE	I don't know. Something. I wanted you to do something. Get mad. Throw things. Cry. Something.
ERNIE	I can't do that.
KATE	No—you go out and buy useless junk and drink beer instead. And I make dinner, and you never show up to eat it. And I go to town and they shake their heads and whisper behind their hands. "Terrible what happened," they say to each other. "Terrible about her husband." Terrible. Terrible.

It's been years . . . it's been a long time, and no one in this town ever forgets.

Pause.

ERNIE   Can I have a piece of that china?

KATE   Why?

ERNIE   Just give me a piece.

KATE goes and takes a piece from the crate and gives it to ERNIE. He throws it into the yard.

There. I threw something. *(pause)* I miss him, too, Kate. It's just my way. I'm just . . . well, I'm no good at these things. I'm better at talking to the guys at the auction hall, saying, "How about that weather," and "This sure is a nice place."

KATE   Promise me no more auctions, Ernie. No more junk, no more drinking. *(Pause as she waits for a response, she has a realization.)* You can't, can you.

Pause.

ERNIE   I went to this auction to get something for you.

KATE   I don't need any dishes /

ERNIE   Not the dishes. Something else. *(ERNIE fishes in his pocket and produces a flashy costume jewellery brooch.)* Here.

KATE   *(taking the brooch)* How did you /

ERNIE   I knew you always liked it. We'd see Mrs. Cranch in town and you'd always talk about that beautiful brooch she had, and how her husband had bought it at a fancy jewellery store in the city. They were selling off her estate today.

KATE   I can't wear this. Everyone knows who it belonged to.

ERNIE   I thought you liked it.

Pause as KATE and ERNIE consider each other.

I love you, Katie.

KATE   *(emotionally)* I know you do, Ernie, I know you do.

KATE looks at ERNIE and pins the brooch onto her dress. She walks over to the screen door and unlatches it. ERNIE comes in the house. ERNIE and KATE regard each other. ERNIE puts his hands on either side of KATE's face and kisses her.

ERNIE   You take my breath away.

The lights fade to black.

Air Apparent
by Sandra Dempsey

One of the forgotten, Aisling is losing her grasp on the periphery of society as she struggles with the after-effects of 9/11. Her health is destroyed by the grey dust, she can't even keep up with her meagre dog walking, and she is left as one of the thousands of *insignificants*, with terrible, insidious internal injuries, struggling for every breath.

Air Apparent was performed in student productions in several locations, including Washington, DC.

CHARACTER LIST

Aisling [ASH-zling] is twenty-eight and has bad lungs. She is sickly and constantly cold, and her poor lung function and hypoxia worsen throughout the play.

A NOTE ON PRODUCTION

If an oxygen tank prop is used, it should remain hidden behind her. When specified later, she should step aside to reveal it, connect the cannula tubing to it, and turn it on. If no oxygen tank is used, the actor may simply leave the connection end of the cannula tubing in her pocket when she puts the nasal prongs on. Colour-blind casting is welcome and encouraged.

...

With a keen sense of drama and a formidable wit, Sandra Dempsey writes complex plays inhabited by articulate, richly drawn, and emotional characters. Uncompromising and vital; powerful, compassionate, and impassioned. Her award-winning produced and published works include the full-length plays *Flying To Glory*, *Enigma*, *Armagideon*, and *D'Arcy*; and short plays such as *Barbie & Ken*, *Casualties*, *Rosa's Lament*, *Orders*, *Fat Cans*, *Legacy*, *A Wing and a Prayer*, and *But We All Have That Here*. Her latest full-length play, *Wings To Victory*, dramatizes the amazing Allied women flyers in WWII. Sandra is also a popular, dynamic performance-reader of her works.

Air Apparent

AISLING

The air was fine. They said so. The air was positively good. The EPA said they did test after test after test—it was apparent; perfectly all clear, so the air was fine. Going on fifteen years ago.

And all I did was live in my little half-studio room over a guy and his family that runs the bodega downstairs. Half dog walking, half social assistance—it's all I can do to give the guy some rent every month. Not a bad guy—poor, but nice family, cute little kids. I acted tough, but he figured I should still be a kid being that I was just fourteen. We're all illegal, just from different directions. Him and his wife came up from South America and I'm from Toronto, totally illegal. He *works* like a dog and I can't believe people pay me money to *walk theirs*.

In terms of the map, we were just off Cedar Street, right next to the financial district. Half his business came from there. For all their ten-grand suits, you wouldn't believe how many of those high-finance snobs would rather hoof it over here to the bodega for their coffee, just to save a buck or two. I've even seen a guy pull out some trendy coffee joint's cup and pour the cheap stuff into it, just to maintain his ego.

Mere blocks from the pile. Two jetliners, a sad rain of jumpers, and about a half-dozen buildings all became a giant boiling, belching cloud. It engulfed us, inches thick of grey—we tried desperately to see, to think, to move, to breathe. That *air*—impossible.

We weren't some of the hundreds of guys digging in that toxic rubble with their bare hands, trying to unearth the mangled scraps of body parts or whatever the hell they were looking for. But day after day, me and the family downstairs, we chewed the same *air*. *Air* that covered everything, not just outside but *inside*—*in* our apartments, and *in* his store, everywhere downstairs; trying to clean up that damn grey dust that lay everywhere—the windows, the sills, in the curtains, even on the kitchen stove, *inside* the microwave, *inside* his food coolers—dust as caustic as oven cleaner. It just kept accumulating over and over. Even the apples and onions and potatoes in his bins—covered in the dust, day after day. And even when you were positive it was all clean, next day the horrible grey crap was back.

Our lungs full of the dust, the debris, the asbestos, the lead, the fibreglass, the plastics, the jet fuel, the transformer oils, the Freons, the PCPs, the POCs, the dioxins, the mercury, the carcinogens, the super-heated glass, the pulverized concrete, the hundreds of toxic chemical compounds, the flesh, the blood, the shit, the piss, the spit and the tears.

> *She coughs violently. Hereafter, she gradually becomes very short of breath and begins to gasp for air as she speaks, progressively fragmenting her sentences to enable her breaths.*

I remember wandering around and finally getting taken somewhere to get interviewed, assessed, tested, to see if I'd *suffered any detriments from events of that day*. Forms and questions and *proof-you-are*, *determination-you-ain't*. When the official rejection was cast and I tried to appeal, I couldn't get any further because I couldn't supply *proof* that I didn't have bad lungs *before* that day, that date, that sunny blue-sky date. No compensation, no free treatment or care. Either the growing medical bills for real good care and drugs would be my responsibility, or I settle for free junk treatment from the junk docs at the junk hospital.

I finally got some nurse to let me see my chest X-ray and CT scans, all lit up and hanging right next to tests from normal, healthy ones. Even a blind monkey could see the differences. Where the right lung was supposed to show up nice and clear and looking black with all sorts of invisible healthy air inside, mine was all honeycombed with big white blotches, through all three lobes.

> *As her breathing and speaking become more laboured, she hooks herself up to an oxygen tank—she puts the nasal cannula prongs into her nostrils, then loops the tubing around her ears and tightens it under her chin. She turns on the silent oxygen flow and pauses to slow her breathing.*

My two left lung lobes were full of white, irregular ridges, like some kind of grotesque moonscape. Who the hell knows about having five lung lobes? I always thought, a lung on the left, a lung on the right, that makes two. Now we speak of lobes. And now we speak of new terms: nodules, lymphoma, tumours, lesions, tuberculosis, cancer.

But we thank God the government was *Johnny-on-the-spot*, testing and re-testing that air. None of us were expecting medals for taking a deep breath. All we wanted was for the *experts* to find out how safe or unsafe that air was and to let us know and to fix it. And they assured us that we were safe—officially, unequivocally, perfectly unsullied and positively, not-even-a-home-renovation-dust-mask-required *safe*. That's peace of mind, they said. A piece of *whose* mind, I said. It was at least one thing we didn't have to worry about, they said.

Why, even ol' *Rudy Giuliani* himself, with his giant posse of millionaire administrators following everywhere he went, was marching around without so much as a hanky to his nose. If *Rudy* could breathe, so could we all. But let me tell you, as soon as the TV cameras stopped rolling, his body guards were doing the breathing *for him*. I mean, he couldn't get into his air-conditioned limo fast enough. And for the rest of us lowly residents? Well, *Rudy* could say the EPA had *assured* him the air was fine, and not even the dogs were in danger.

> *The fragmentation of sentences worsens progressively as she must take a second or third breath in between phrases and words, often at disjointed, irregular points.*

Now *I* can assure *them* that I can't breathe without an oxygen tank. I can't keep from turning blue without extra O_2. I can't speak without gasping on every sentence. All the time, I cough up tons of horrible, disgusting, thick, sticky junk—you can actually see the flecks of dirty black oil or whatever the hell it is all streaked through. That's all we do, me and the bodega family, we can hear each other every night, cough and cough and cough. It's getting worse and more frequent every day. Yesterday, I coughed and there was some blood.

No more dogs to walk. I can't keep up with any dog anymore. And all those rescue dogs, some three hundred of them were deployed, they all got sick and died. Somebody said they even read the dogs' names at the anniversaries. Fifteen years, and nobody's doing any crowdfunding to help us. They found megabucks to build a big, new, shiny target for the next attack, but nobody ever thought about us fall-outs—us *uninsured* fall-outs. When one of us croaks, nobody ever reads our names in front of respectful dignitaries. None of our names will ever appear on any commemorative brass memorial.

> *She stops to rest, bending at the waist with her hands on her knees; this allows the weight of her chest muscles to fall away from her lungs and give her slightly more space to inflate them. She tries to recover her energy and slow her breathing.*

I can't hardly make it down the stairs, the full three floors. The bodega guy and his family moved to a new place and I got to come along, maybe to see who's gonna outlive who. It's way smaller, still one room but even smaller than my first—I can touch both walls with my hands, but that's less to clean, right? Nobody comes anymore anyway, and except for going to the junk doctors and getting more and more tests, I can't go out at all anymore. I just can't do it.

> *She straightens, and as her agitation increases, she gets more short of breath, gasping.*

The tissue in my nose is damaged. I can't smell anymore. My eyes are red and burn all the time. They got so dry and damaged, my tears can't come out normal anymore—the *nasolacrimal duct* is damaged, so now tears can only come straight down through my nose. Who the hell knows about *nasolacrimal ducts*? I'm twenty-eight, I have the lungs of a ninety-year-old, and the only way I can cry is through my damn nose.

> *She tries in vain to regain her composure, gulping gasps of air.*

So me, and the bodega guy, and his family, we're all going to be perfectly A-okay. The air was fine, positively good. *Rudy* himself had the EPA doing test after test after test—perfectly all clear, so the air was fine. And we're all of us perfectly normal—each and every one of us, a perfectly normal *air apparent* to our own very limited near future.

> *Her breathing becomes loud and laboured, continues into the blackout, and then abruptly stops.*
>
> *Blackout.*

Summer's End
by Francine Dick

Three sisters inherit the family cottage but young Kristen has different plans for it than her much older half-sisters, Carla and Sandy.

Summer's End premiered at Toronto's Alumnae Theatre, directed by Kerri MacDonald and starring Candi Zell, Heather Mann, and Alyssa Faith Owsiany.

CHARACTER LIST

Kristin
Carla
Sandy

...

Francine Dick was born in Toronto, where she still lives. *As Large As Alone* premiered at the New Ideas Festival in Toronto in 2006 and was also presented at the Last Frontier Theatre Conference in Valdez, Alaska, in 2008 and the Great Plains Theatre Conference in Omaha, Nebraska, in 2009. *Living In Permafrost* was presented at the Last Frontier Theatre Conference in 2010. *Preparing for Passover* was presented at the Great Plains Theatre Conference in 2011, Big Ideas at the Alumnae Theatre in 2012, and at the Daylesford Theatre in Hamilton, Bermuda, in 2013. Francine's other plays include *Down Memory Lane* (She Speaks, International Centre for Women Playwrights, 2007) and *On the Street* (Nuit Blanche, Toronto, 2007). *Wedding Night In Canada* was a hit at the Toronto Fringe Festival in 2010. Her short story, "Pflegespulung," won the Writers' Union of Canada 2010 Postcard Story Competition. A single mom of three amazing kids and a strong community activist, Francine believes in giving back as much as we receive.

Summer's End

Three women are sitting on a dock. There are two deck chairs and a patio table. KRISTIN, *twenty-four, small and slight, sits at the edge of the dock with her feet in the water.* CARLA, *fifty, sits in a deck chair while* SANDY, *forty-seven, sits on the dock. Both are sturdy, middle-aged women. Beside* CARLA *is a hard, opaque case that carries official papers.*

KRISTIN	The water's warm this year.
SANDY	It's late August. The water's always warm by now.
KRISTIN	It's quiet, too.
SANDY	Most people are away. They'll be back over Labour Day.
KRISTIN	Is that a new boathouse at the MacDonald's cottage?
CARLA	MacDougall. Not so new. About four years old.
KRISTIN	Wow, has it been that long since I was up here?
SANDY	Six years. You were here for their twentieth anniversary party.

KRISTIN	Oh yeah, I remember. I've been so busy since then with school and now work.
CARLA	You were lucky to get that great job, straight out of university.
KRISTIN	I like to think it was more a result of my great resumé, rather than luck.
CARLA	I'm sure it was. You're a very smart woman. You'd be an asset to any company.
KRISTIN	I think so, too. It IS a great job, with lots of potential.
SANDY	And in Montreal. What a fabulous city for a young woman.
KRISTIN	Yeah, all that French immersion paid off.
SANDY	So, I guess you won't be coming here very much.
KRISTIN	Oh, I don't know. I do get vacation time.
SANDY	And you'd spend two weeks of your precious summer holidays here?
KRISTIN	Maybe.
CARLA	You haven't been up in six years. You hated coming here. You only came because Nicole forced you to come.
SANDY	And she never cared for it much.
KRISTIN	Yes she did. She and Daddy had lots of fun together.
SANDY	Only when the Garrisons were over for cards.
CARLA	She'd get into the gin and start flirting with Mr. Garrison.
KRISTIN	She did not.
CARLA	*(mimicking)* Oh, Eric, I just love your new motorboat. Why don't you take me for a ride in it around the lake?
SANDY	Disgusting. Poor Daddy.
KRISTIN	She loved him.

CARLA	Who? Eric Garrison?
KRISTIN	No, our father.
SANDY	Funny way of showing it.
KRISTIN	And she did like coming here.
CARLA	Oh come on, Kristin. She hated this place. Daddy tried everything to make it enjoyable for her. He put in the satellite TV . . .
SANDY	Whirlpool bathtub . . .
CARLA	Dishwasher . . .
SANDY	Brand new furniture, including that very expensive mattress.
CARLA	But nothing worked.
KRISTIN	All right. She didn't like it. She's a city girl. She can't help it.
SANDY	She'll never come back here.
KRISTIN	Well, I don't know.
SANDY	I do. She won't come.
CARLA	It's why Daddy left the cottage to the three of us instead of her.
KRISTIN	I know. That was sweet of him.
CARLA	It was foolish. What do you want with this cottage?
KRISTIN	I own a third.
SANDY	Let us buy your share.
KRISTIN	We've been through this. No.
CARLA	We'll give you a good price. Market value.
SANDY	That's a lot of money for a twenty-four-year-old. You could buy a small condo in Montreal. The cottage is worth quite a lot.
KRISTIN	And it'll be worth more in a decade.
SANDY	How do you know?
KRISTIN	I know. I read the papers. All those retiring baby boomers are looking for summer homes.

SANDY	But you could take the money and invest it now. It'll appreciate more than this property.
KRISTIN	With the way the markets have been? I did study business, you know.
CARLA	We know. That's why it makes no sense for you to refuse our buyout.
KRISTIN	I like this cottage.
SANDY	You hate this cottage. Every time you came up you complained.
CARLA	The bugs, the boredom. You never even learned to swim.
KRISTIN	But I'm more mature now. My attitude has changed. And the cottage is a connection I have with Daddy.
CARLA	That valuable coin collection he left you is a stronger connection.
SANDY	Listen, Kristin. Our father bought this cottage fifty years ago with our mother.
CARLA	Not yours. Ours.
SANDY	She loved being here and so did we. Carla and I spent every summer together with our mother at this cottage.
CARLA	Even in university we worked in town so we could be here. We love this place.
SANDY	This is our heritage. Let us have it.
KRISTIN	Daddy left it to the three of us. We all own it. And I get to use it a third of the time.
SANDY	You'll be here four months of the year?
KRISTIN	I might. I have a lot of flexibility with my job.
CARLA	Not that much. What will you do with four months?
KRISTIN	I don't know. Maybe I'll rent it out.
CARLA	You can't do that.

KRISTIN | Who says I can't? Nothing in Daddy's will says I can't. It just says we share it equally, one third each. It doesn't stipulate what I can or can't do with my share.

CARLA | You'll have to pay property taxes.

SANDY | Which are only getting more and more expensive. And you'll have to contribute to the maintenance.

KRISTIN | Who says so?

SANDY | If you're an owner you have to pay your share.

KRISTIN | No I don't. Daddy's will just said I get a third share. It didn't say anything about paying taxes or maintenance.

CARLA | You think Sandy and I should pay it all?

KRISTIN | Why not? You obviously want the cottage more than anything.

CARLA | You little shit. We'll let it run down to decrease the value.

KRISTIN | No you won't.

SANDY | We'll burn it down.

KRISTIN | Oh, that's a great idea, Sandy. Destroy your childhood and go to jail for arson.

CARLA | We're offering you a good price, Kristin. It's more than fair. You got a lot of other things from Daddy and you'll get whatever your mother leaves you. Why won't you let Sandy and me have this?

KRISTIN | I already told you. This is an investment in my future.

SANDY | You're just trying to get back at us.

KRISTIN | Oh, and why would I want to do that, Sandy?

SANDY | Because you couldn't get rid of our mother.

KRISTIN | What? She got rid of herself. She died. Long before I was born.

SANDY | Daddy sold our family home so he and Nicole could have a fresh start.

CARLA	A two-bedroom condo so there wasn't even room for us.
SANDY	But he didn't sell the cottage. And our mother's presence was everywhere.
KRISTIN	I'll say. The snowshoes over the fireplace. The lame board games. Those godawful rugs my mom finally threw out.
SANDY	Without telling us. Kristin, Carla and I made those together with our mother. Hand-hooked.
KRISTIN	Yeah, and they looked like they belonged in a hooker's house. Sorry, sisters, but your mother had pretty awful taste.
CARLA	Pushing your luck, aren't you, Kristin?
KRISTIN	Well, nothing you can do about it. I own a third.
CARLA	We can make you sell.
KRISTIN	Really, Carla, and how do you propose doing that?
CARLA	Sign the papers or we'll throw you in the lake.
KRISTIN	I know I haven't been here for awhile but I do remember the water at the end of the dock barely reaching my waist.
CARLA	You didn't notice.
KRISTIN	Notice what?
SANDY	The dock.
KRISTIN	What about the dock?
SANDY	It's longer.
CARLA	A lot longer.
KRISTIN	*(shifts and looks around at the dock)* Oh, yes, it is. When did this happen?
CARLA	Right after their twentieth anniversary. Your mother wanted a powerboat. So Daddy bought her one.
SANDY	He needed to extend the dock into deeper water

to accommodate it. Must be twelve feet off the end.

CARLA   Closer to fifteen I think.

KRISTIN slowly gets up and tries to back away from the edge of the dock, but SANDY and CARLA block her way.

Where are you going, Kristin?

KRISTIN   Let me go.

SANDY   Where are you going?

KRISTIN   Back to the cottage.

SANDY   Why? You hate it there.

CARLA   We cancelled the satellite TV, so it's really boring now.

KRISTIN   I need to pee.

CARLA   Sign the papers, Kristin.

KRISTIN   No.

CARLA   Sign the papers or we'll throw you in the lake.

KRISTIN   You wouldn't.

CARLA   No. Wanna try us?

CARLA nods to SANDY. They each grab hold of KRISTIN's upper arms and drag her to the edge of the dock, pushing her upper body over the water.

KRISTIN   *(flailing, trying to back up, hysterical)* Let me go, stop it, help, put me down, please let me go.

CARLA and SANDY drop her on the dock.

CARLA   Sign the papers, Kristin.

SANDY   Sign them or we'll do it.

KRISTIN   You'd murder me? You could live with that?

CARLA   I'd sleep like a baby.

KRISTEN   I'll claim I signed the papers under duress.

CARLA   Oh yeah, that chunk of change you're getting is so stressful.

KRISTIN	I'll get a lawyer to stop the process.
CARLA	I already told Daddy's lawyer you were anxious to sell. Everything is set to go. All we need is your signature and then I'm off to the land office.
KRISTIN	No, I won't. And you won't. You'd never get away with it. They'd find out. They'd know you were here.
CARLA	Oh yes, we are here, but we got here after you.
SANDY	*(the next few lines are spoken with feigned concern)* Oh, Carla, look, there's Kristin's car. She made it up before us.
CARLA	But she's not in the cottage.
SANDY	Maybe she went for a walk.
CARLA	Oh no, Sandy, look, there's her towel on the dock.
SANDY	She probably forgot about the dock extension.
CARLA	And she can't swim.
SANDY	Oh no, Carla! What should we do?
CARLA	You call the police. I'll go look for her in the water, like the good sister I am.
KRISTIN	You wouldn't.
SANDY	We would.
CARLA	And if we did that we wouldn't even have to buy you out.

CARLA *and* SANDY *smile at each other.* KRISTIN *makes a dash to escape, but is once again cut off.* CARLA *and* SANDY *pick her up, one woman holding her ankles, the other under her arms. They start to swing her over the edge of the dock.* KRISTIN *screams hysterically.*

| KRISTIN | Put me down, put me down. I'll sign, just put me down. |

CARLA *and* SANDY *drop her and she crumples, sobbing, to the dock.* CARLA *takes the official looking document out of the plastic case.*

SANDY	Sign the deed, Kristin!
CARLA	*(CARLA holds the document and a pen out to KRISTIN.)* Sign it!

KRISTIN, still sobbing, takes the pen from CARLA.

Sign here.

(turns the page)

And here.

(turns the page)

And one more right here. Very good. You should have your cheque within the week.

KRISTIN, still sobbing, runs off. CARLA and SANDY sit down on the edge of the dock, lean back against their hands and dangle their feet.

CARLA	The water really is warm this year.
SANDY	We should go for a swim.
CARLA	As soon as we get back from town.

END

Pee & Qs
A *short play*
by Josh Downing

Three men find themselves in an awkward position when faced with the rules of the workplace washroom.

Pee & Qs premiered at Gay Play Day at Alumnae Theatre in Toronto, directed by Josh Downing, with set design by Ben Stansfield, and featuring Ryan Egan as Hank, Michael Lake as Paul, and Joseph Yeboah, Jr. as Steve.

CHARACTER LIST

Hank	Senior Manager
Paul	Junior Manager
Steve	Office Associate

SETTING

A men's bathroom behind three urinals. The urinals can be as simple as three cardboard drawings on a simple stand.

TIME

Present

...

Josh Downing originally studied in the Douglas College Performing Arts Program and more recently at George Brown College, taking the playwriting class to refresh his writing skills. *Pee & Qs* was his first short play to hit the stage, premiering at the Gay Play Day festival and remounted for the HamilTEN Festival of 10-Minute Plays. Josh attended the InspiraTO Playwriting Academy, which produced his play *Intersection*, and he also directed Caity-Shea Violette's *Save the Date*, which won the Blue Show Audience Favourite award. Josh's newest play *The _ _ _ Wedding* premiered at the Gay Play Day festival in 2015.

Pee & Qs

Lights come up on the backs of three urinals standing close together. HANK, wearing a white shirt, a tie, and black pants, enters and stops before moving to one of the urinals.

HANK

(to the audience) Why did the homo cross the road? What is your marital status? Hobbies and associations? Not exactly the questions you get on the job application, but they want to know. Not the punchline. How you react. What is your response? Did your heart rate go up a little bit? Are you flush? Will you laugh or will you pull a rainbow flag out of your right back pocket and wave it defiantly? Chances are good if you chuckle and say that's a good one, you'll get the job here whether or not you actually have the flag in your pocket. As long as you keep it there.

HANK takes his place at the urinal on the left side.

PAUL, also wearing black pants, a white shirt, and a tie, enters and stops to address the audience.

PAUL

Paruresis. Piss shy. Stage fright. Shy bladder. Doesn't matter what you call it. It's real and it hurts. If you gotta go, then you gotta go. But I wonder how much of that is just plain fear. You know the kind of fear that causes people to make up rules for public washrooms. Like the rule about which urinal to use. First in always takes one of the urinals on either end. Second in takes the urinal on the opposite end. Easy, right? In the three-urinal scenario the third man is out of luck. So he has to make a choice, quickly find a toilet stall or go directly to the sink and start washing his hands, making it look like that was what he meant to do. Of course he can't spend too much time in front of the mirror because that's how rumours start. If he's lucky though, one of the urinals will become available and he can stop washing or fixing his hair and move to that urinal, as if he just decided, Oh right, I might as well go pee while I am here. If he's not so lucky and there is a lot of paruresis going on, then it's back to his desk he goes. So what are we afraid of? Afraid of another man looking at us while we are at our most vulnerable? Fly open, dick in hand. Afraid of not making large enough splashing sounds? Afraid of curiosity, peeking? And what? Liking it?

PAUL *takes the urinal at the opposite end of* HANK. *Both men stand rigid, staring forward.*

STEVE, *dressed in the same clothes as the other two enters, pauses when he sees that only the centre urinal is available. Then he lunges forward to just do it. Both* HANK *and* PAUL *stick their arms out to block* STEVE *from taking the centre urinal.*

HANK	Whoa!
PAUL	Stop!
STEVE	I gotta go!
HANK	Not so fast.
PAUL	Rules are rules.
STEVE	But I have to!
HANK	Don't be that guy.

STEVE	What guy?
PAUL	The middle-urinal guy.
STEVE	The middle what?
PAUL	Urinal.
STEVE	What do I do then?
HANK	You know the drill.
PAUL	Find a stall.

HANK and PAUL chuckle at that.

| STEVE | Great, thanks for nothing. |

STEVE turns and leaves. HANK and PAUL resume their rigid stances. After a beat, HANK chuckles to himself. PAUL tries not to respond. HANK looks over and gives PAUL a quick smile.

PAUL	What?
HANK	Oh, just something I thought about earlier.
PAUL	Hmmm.
HANK	Why did the homo cross the road?
PAUL	The what? The *what*?
HANK	The homo. Why did he cross the road?
PAUL	I don't think I get it.
HANK	You know, like the chicken.
PAUL	Oh, I know the chicken.
HANK	Then, what?

Pause.

PAUL	You broke number two for that?
HANK	Number two?
PAUL	Number two. No talking at the urinal.
HANK	Well it wasn't really talking.
PAUL	Small talk and stuff counts.
HANK	Small talk doesn't really apply to people like me.

PAUL	People like, what?
HANK	Senior people. Senior managers, executives, presidents, CEOs. We don't have to follow number two if we don't want to.
PAUL	Oh, I hadn't heard that. I mean, I've seen it, just not heard there was an exemption. I wonder why.
HANK	Less fear. We have less to fear. We hold more power in the office so we don't have to worry someone is going to do or say something stupid. So we are allowed to make small talk if we want. We can even talk through stall doors if we want to.
PAUL	Sure.
HANK	What, you sound pissed.
PAUL	No, I'm good.
HANK	Really? You don't sound good.

Pause.

PAUL	I don't think it was appropriate.
HANK	What, the joke?
PAUL	Yes, the joke.
HANK	It's just a joke. Doesn't mean anything.
PAUL	Maybe to you.

Pause.

HANK	Well, sorry.
PAUL	Forget it.

HANK gives PAUL a look, zips up, and leaves abruptly.

Oh hell, finally!

STEVE comes rushing back and heads to the empty urinal at the opposite end of PAUL.

PAUL stiffens up and cringes.

STEVE	Holy crap! And I mean that literally!

PAUL ignores him.

Two stalls out of order and the ones on the next floor up are all full. I found one stall that was available but it looked like the last five guys didn't know how to hit the flush button.

PAUL is getting irritated.

Hey, have you noticed that there is always dried booger on the walls around urinals? I don't get that. This is a building full of business professionals and yet no one seems to be able to find a tissue.

STEVE looks over at PAUL.

You okay?

PAUL   No. I am not okay. Everyone just keeps talking and looking at me while I am trying to pee and it seems like all the rules have just gone down the drain.

STEVE   Oh yeah, the rules. I don't pay attention to them most of the time. People seem to get pretty hung up, but I say, what's your issue, dude!

PAUL   Of course they do. No one wants to be chatting about wall snot while they are trying to piss. And no one wants to be looked at either.

STEVE   What's your issue, dude?

PAUL   Not me. I didn't make up the rules.

STEVE   Then what are you so mad for? Scared I might see your junk?

PAUL   Just stop. I'm not mad about that. It's something else.

STEVE   What then?

PAUL   This place. These rules. Hank.

STEVE   Hank? That supervisor guy?

PAUL   Yeah, him.

STEVE   What did he do now?

PAUL   It's what he said.

STEVE	Like what?
PAUL	It was a joke.
STEVE	Oh, I've heard that he has a sick sense of humour. What was the joke?
PAUL	I don't want to repeat it.
STEVE	Come on.

Pause.

PAUL	Why did the homo cross the road?
STEVE	So, why did he?

Pause.

PAUL	I don't know. He never told me the punchline.
STEVE	What? No punchline?
PAUL	No punchline! But I don't even want to know the punchline.
STEVE	It might have actually been funny.
PAUL	I am pretty sure it would have been offensive. Some people don't want to hear that kind of stuff at work.
STEVE	I'm gay and it didn't bother me.
PAUL	You're what? You're gay?
STEVE	Yeah, so what?
PAUL	So what? That's so freaking crazy offensive. You should be so pissed off.
STEVE	Well, on behalf of the gays from floors ten through fourteen, we thank you for your alliance and defence.
PAUL	I'm not defender of the gays, I am gay!
STEVE	You're gay?
PAUL	Yes!
STEVE	Wow, what are the odds?
PAUL	Well, the odds are pretty good that with people

	like Hank running this place we'll most likely be beaten up in the parking lot or looking for new jobs.
STEVE	Why Hank?
PAUL	He's the homophobe! You know, the "chicken crossing the road" joke. Only the chicken is gay.
STEVE	Hank's got a reputation with the perverse jokes but that would be some pretty dark self-loathing.
PAUL	What do you mean?
STEVE	Uh, he's a homo. He might actually be the one that's crossing the road.

PAUL *is speechless.*

	You didn't know? I see him in the bars all the time. He likes his music eighties-style and his men hairy. You must not get out much. In fact, I don't think I've ever seen you out.
PAUL	I'm a suburban gay. Don't go out much. At all.

PAUL *zips up and walks off.*

STEVE	*(to the audience)* I can piss anywhere. Pretty much. I get it that not everyone can, but I just don't get the rules. I don't get that someone might be afraid of another guy seeing his stuff. I mean, who cares? To be perfectly honest, I'm not really interested in even looking at dick at work. It's gross. I have to work with these guys. I don't want to be picturing his shrivelled up little foreskin every time I hand in a report. I don't need to know if he is a shaker, or a banger, or a wriggler. Just as long as he doesn't splash on me, I'm good.

HANK *walks in, pauses, then takes the urinal at the opposite end of* STEVE.

STEVE	Hey.

HANK *remains rigid and silent.* STEVE *looks over at him.*

HANK	Keep it to yourself.

| STEVE | Oh, don't worry. |
| HANK | Do I look worried? |

Pause.

STEVE	So any big plans for the weekend? Dancing at retro night . . .
HANK	You don't seem to care that we have rules around here, do you?
STEVE	I didn't see them posted anywhere so I thought they were just those flexible kind of rules.
HANK	Not a bad idea. Posting them.
STEVE	Just trying to be friendly.
HANK	Well fraternization is something we do have a posted rule about. So don't get too friendly.
STEVE	I just thought . . .
HANK	No, I don't think you really did think. Look, you better be careful around here. You could find yourself in some trouble. I get that you're young and you like your parties but this is a place of business and we like to keep the personal stuff out. No one wants to hear about your escapades.
STEVE	Hey, that's not fair. I see you out. You're one to talk.
HANK	That's where you are wrong. I don't like to talk. My personal life is my personal life and that's the way it is. As far as I am concerned you and I have never crossed paths, have nothing in common, and if you happen to see me outside this office, don't. I don't know you. You don't know me.
STEVE	Wow. Okay.
HANK	Got it?
STEVE	Got it.

Pause.

I guess Paul was right about you.

STEVE zips up and leaves.

HANK   What's that about Paul? Hey! Hey! Steve?

No answer from STEVE. There is a moment then PAUL enters. PAUL sees HANK and stands back from the urinal.

                You okay back there?

Pause.

                The urinal's free up here.

PAUL   Can I ask you a personal question?

HANK   Depends. Are you going to violate my human rights?

PAUL   Probably.

HANK   Then no. You can't.

Pause.

PAUL   Are you married?

HANK   Not answering.

PAUL   Got any kids?

HANK   Irrelevant.

PAUL   Catch the game on Saturday night?

HANK   What game?

PAUL   Hah! Wrong answer! Every straight guy knows every game and every team and every puck or ball that was ever shot, smacked, hooked, and passed into a goal.

HANK   So. What did that just prove? That I don't follow sports? So what?

PAUL   Tell me you weren't dancing to Madonna with a bearded guy on Saturday night.

HANK   It wasn't Madonna . . .

Pause.

Look, it's none of your business what I do on my own time. Why are all the guys around here so fucking nosy?

Pause.

PAUL steps up to the urinal right next to HANK.

PAUL	Are you uncomfortable?
HANK	Yes.
PAUL	Good.
HANK	What the hell are you doing?

PAUL looks right at HANK, then looks down at HANK's crotch, then back to his face.

PAUL   Crossing the road, Hank. Crossing the road.

Fade to black.

The Prisoner
by Jennifer Fawcett

In an unnamed country, a widow comes to find out what happened to her husband and warn her husband's guard of the fate that awaits him.

CHARACTER LIST

Woman   The widow of a former guard, poor, desperate, smart. Any age, any ethnicity.

Guard   A prison guard, military (undefined); believes in his authority. Any age, any ethnicity.

Another guard   Dressed identically to the first. Any age, any ethnicity.

SETTING

A bare room containing two doors on opposite sides of the room, a table, and a chair. One door leads to the outside, the other leads to the prisoner's cell.

...

Jennifer Fawcett is a playwright, actor, and the co-artistic director of Working Group Theatre. She is the winner of the 2015 National New Play Network's Smith Prize for Political Theater, a 2014 New England Foundation for the Arts' National Theater Project Award (with Working Group Theatre), the 2008 National Science Playwriting Award (The Kennedy Centre American College Theater Festival), and she was nominated for the 2013 Steinberg/ATCA New Play Award. Her work has been commissioned and produced by Hancher Auditorium (APAP/University of Iowa), Riverside Theatre (Iowa City), Available Light Theatre (Columbus), Tennessee Women's Theater Project (Nashville), MusicIC (Iowa City), the Drilling Company (New York), the Adirondack Theatre Festival (Glens Falls, NY), the Alcyone Festival (Chicago), the Source Festival (Washington, DC), and in festivals across Canada including SummerWorks and the Rhubarb Festival. A graduate of the University of Iowa's MFA Program in Playwrighting, the Playwrights Workshop, she was the NNPN playwright-in-residence at Curious Theatre (Denver). Her work has been developed at Nightwood Theatre (Toronto) as part of the Groundswell Festival, at Berkeley Repertory Theatre (Berkeley, CA) as part of the Ground Floor Summer Residency Lab, at the Banff Playwrights Colony, the Lark (New York City), Penn State, Portland Stage Company (Portland, ME), Palm Beach Dramaworks (West Palm Beach, FL), and many more. She currently lives in Iowa.

The Prisoner

A GUARD *sits at a small table in front of the cell door.*

A WOMAN *enters from the opposite door.*

The GUARD *doesn't acknowledge her at first. He continues to read papers from a file on his desk. The* WOMAN *waits.*

WOMAN   My husband used to sit where you are.

No response.

                  Every day except Sundays.

No response.

                  He'd tell me about the people who came to this door.

                  Mostly women.

                  Is it still mostly women?

No response.

                  Jacob. That was his name, not yours—or is it?

GUARD   No.

WOMAN   No. That would be too much of a coincidence.

That chair was his chair. Be careful, there's a rough bit on one of the back slats. It would sometimes catch his suit if he got up quickly.

Sometimes, with this job, that is required. Quickness. No matter how long you've been sitting you must always be ready to spring up. He always tried to keep his desk as clear as possible, so papers wouldn't go flying all over the place.

And, of course, the fewer papers on the desk, the fewer distractions.

GUARD   I have the papers that I need. No more, no less.

WOMAN   Where were you stationed before here?

GUARD   At another door.

WOMAN   Outside?

GUARD   Yes.

WOMAN   All the other doors are outside, so I didn't need to ask. It's funny how we do that.

No response.

You must be relieved then to have my husband's job. What a good thing for you. Out of the weather.

GUARD   And the crowds.

WOMAN   Crowds?

GUARD   They don't listen.

WOMAN   Not in here though.

GUARD   No. In here it is mostly women.

WOMAN   In here we listen.

Well, that's good then. Yes, Jacob would talk about the women coming to his desk. He was always shy around women, but I think he enjoyed their presence. Of course he wouldn't show them that.

Maybe you're enjoying talking to me?

The GUARD *remains silent.*

Hmm, yes. Well. Of course you can't say.

Beat.

Is that his file there?

GUARD   His file was destroyed. That is the policy.

WOMAN   I'm well aware of the policies. I'm not like the other women who come to your desk, you know. I have an understanding of the policies. But surely there must be some sort of record you keep. For history. Or for the sake of knowing who and how and when.

You will remember my coming today. You'll create a file for me.

The GUARD *is silent.*

Is that *my* file then?

There are many pages, it seems. Why are there so many pages? It makes me feel like I must have a more exciting life than I actually do. May I see it?

GUARD   No.

WOMAN   But if it's mine.

GUARD   Then there's no reason for you to see it.

WOMAN   I didn't know I had a file. To think, I am being recorded. My days pass in the usual way but they don't disappear. Someone is watching. I need to be sure I do things worthy of my file.

GUARD   This is a joke?

WOMAN   No. I'm quite serious.

GUARD   Oh.

I couldn't tell if that was supposed to be a joke.

WOMAN   It wasn't. Never joke about a file.

I'm not very good at jokes. I was always glad I wasn't a man because of that. Men have to be able to joke. Or talk about sports. Or politics. I guess I could have learned about one of those subjects, if I were a man. Maybe it comes easier to you. It's become a rule because of the expectation. It's the way we naturally are, or enough of us are at least, that it comes to be expected that we'll all be that way. I wouldn't know how to talk to other men if I were a man. It's different as a woman, don't you think?

GUARD   I wouldn't know.

WOMAN   No. Of course you wouldn't. But you can imagine. I try to imagine what it would be like to be a man—to be a guard, for example.

GUARD   There is no point in imagining. You will never be a man, or a guard. Leave it at that.

He takes an orange out of his pocket and begins to peel it.

She watches him.

WOMAN   There was a woman who would come with oranges. Once a month she'd come and give an orange to my husband. She always had oranges even when they weren't in season. At night, we'd eat the orange together and try to imagine where it had come from.

GUARD   Why did he let her keep returning?

WOMAN   He liked the oranges. And . . .

GUARD   And?

WOMAN   I am the wife of a guard. There are things I know that other women don't.

The GUARD begins to eat his orange. He's methodical about this, like it's a ritual of some sort.

She watches him.

Of course the oranges she brought were meant for her husband. They say we're allowed to bring the prisoners food. Just like that one you're eating now.

GUARD   It's a sin to let food go to waste.

WOMAN   Jacob would say the same thing.

And the woman knew. When she would give him

the orange, she would say, "for my husband." She didn't say, "an orange for my husband." It was the gesture that was for him, the act of coming here, of bringing food. It's not important who eats it in the end. This way she will be able to go home and imagine him here. She doesn't know the room you guard is empty.

The GUARD *stands suddenly.*

WOMAN	Be careful on the chair. Your suit.
GUARD	Why are you here?
WOMAN	I'm giving you plenty to write about for my file, aren't I. You'll remember me.

Beat.

I don't have any oranges to give you.

GUARD	You shouldn't be here.
WOMAN	Where else would I go?
GUARD	You have a home. You shouldn't have come here today.
WOMAN	I came to see you.
GUARD	For a guard's wife, you are dangerously ignorant.
WOMAN	You aren't guarding prisoners. There aren't any prisoners. You're guarding us—the ones left behind. The mourners who don't know they're mourners.
GUARD	Why would I do that?
WOMAN	Because it would all fall apart if you didn't.
GUARD	Your children will lose both their parents.
WOMAN	Are you married?
GUARD	That's none of your business.
WOMAN	You must be. They only give this position to married men. The unmarried ones would just shoot us, or try to fuck us, but the married ones are more careful. You're peeking into your own future.

GUARD	My future? No, not mine.
WOMAN	Someday this will be your wife coming here. She'll bring something maybe. Something she'll know you would have liked.
GUARD	I'll forbid her to come. I'll tell her the truth.
WOMAN	But you haven't told her yet?
GUARD	No.
WOMAN	My husband told me.
	He would have liked you. You're very similar.
GUARD	I'll tell her the truth so she won't come. She won't be one of your pathetic group, waiting in line to come in and speak to me, begging and crying. She won't have a file.
WOMAN	You love her very much.
GUARD	Of course I do. She's my wife.
WOMAN	Then you must let her come here.
GUARD	I won't lie to her.
WOMAN	No, don't lie to her.
GUARD	If she knew the truth, she wouldn't come. I don't think you know even though you say you do.
WOMAN	You should pretend that I am your wife.
GUARD	You are not my wife.
WOMAN	I said pretend, just for now. Speak to me the way you will want the next one to speak to her.
GUARD	There will be no next one.
WOMAN	There is always a next one. Because they have moved you inside, because you guard the room that never holds a prisoner, because you eat the oranges, pretend I am your wife. What would you have the next man say to her?
GUARD	I will not pretend this.
WOMAN	It is a kindness, I think. You will want him to show her kindness.

GUARD   Yes.

WOMAN   What would you like to say to her?

GUARD   You must not come here.

WOMAN   She will say, "There is nothing else for me to do. It is through this that I can imagine you are in that room."

GUARD   But I am not. If I am not here, then I am not in that room. I am gone. This is the last stop.

WOMAN   For me then. Pretend for me.

                    Please.

            Beat.

            He sits back down. The game begins.

                    Jacob, are you warm?

GUARD   Yes.

WOMAN   Are you at peace?

GUARD   Yes.

WOMAN   Was it fast? Were they merciful?

GUARD   It was fast. There was no pain.

            Ending the game.

                    How will I tell her this?

WOMAN   You've told me. That's enough.

GUARD   But you are not my wife.

WOMAN   And you are not my husband. My husband said these words to another woman and your wife will hear them from another man. It doesn't matter who says them, it is saying them and hearing them that helps us.

GUARD   But how do you know—just because I say it was fast and there was no pain—how do you know that's true?

WOMAN   Because you are the one who did it. Just as the next man who speaks to your wife will tell her how you died.

GUARD   Get out of here. I don't want to play this game of yours.

WOMAN   When I leave, another man will come in. He has been relieved of outside duty. He wears the same uniform you do.

GUARD   Not yet.

WOMAN   He's waiting outside. I asked him to wait. For the sake of your wife.

He breaks down. She goes to him.

Shh. It will be fast. And he'll tell your wife. Shh now.

She leaves the room through the outside door, closing it behind her.

The GUARD *stares at the door.*

A moment, and then the outside door opens.

Another GUARD *steps in.*

The two GUARDS *face each other.*

Blackout.

END

This Isn't Toronto
by Catherine Frid

A mother and her grown daughter are forced to confront a life-changing crossroad in their relationship.

This Isn't Toronto was created with a group of Wellington County seniors as part of *Our Voices: Senior Selfies*, a show funded by the New Horizons for Seniors Program about the realities of being a senior today. It featured the following cast and creative team:

Actors	Catherine Frid, Gloria Nye
Director	Dale Hamilton
Stage Manager	Ed Langevin
Lighting Design	McBride Hunter
Sound Design	Joe Brenner
Projection Design	John Cripton

CHARACTER LIST

Val	a woman, about sixty
Carolyn	Val's daughter, late twenties

...

Catherine Frid's plays include *AfterWhys*, commissioned by the Suicide Awareness Council of Wellington-Dufferin, *Half Full* (Mixed Company Theatre school tour), *Thistlepatch* (Law and Curated Body Conference and others), *SKI Club* (with composer Frank Horvat, Big Ideas Reading Festival), *Our Voices: Senior Selfies* (Eden Mills), *Burying Toni* (Alumnae Theatre), *Over The Edge* (New Ideas Festival, Key City Public Theatre, WA), *The Bold Canadian: Laura Secord and Her Legacy* (Arts and Letters Club), *Homegrown* (SummerWorks and others), *GuineaPigging* (Alumnae Theatre), *Dead Cat Bounce* (Toronto Fringe and others), and a number of short works. Catherine was artist-in-residence at Osgoode Hall Law School in 2014, and playwright-in-residence at Mixed Company Theatre in 2015.

This Isn't Toronto

VAL's living room. CAROLYN lets herself in through the front door. She's holding a rolled-up newspaper. CAROLYN hesitates and then hides the newspaper, perhaps under a chair. She hesitates again, then goes back out and rings the doorbell. VAL enters, holding a cup of coffee. She answers the door.

VAL   Hi, honey, come on in. The door's open. I'm working from home today, doing an evaluation.

CAROLYN enters.

CAROLYN   'Morning, Mom. I saw your car in the driveway.

VAL   Do you want coffee?

CAROLYN   No, thanks.

VAL   I found Keith's science kit, it's up in his room.

CAROLYN   *(confused)* Keith's what?

VAL   The old science kit you wanted to show your grade fours. Isn't that why you came by? I Windexed the magnifying glass for you. Carolyn, did you see my newspaper? It wasn't here when I got up.

VAL *looks out a window.*

CAROLYN	Nope.
VAL	I don't understand it. The delivery girl is usually so reliable. I hope the Bolton's smelly, slobbering retriever didn't "retrieve" my paper. You know me and dogs. *(She looks at her watch and does a double take.)* Aren't you supposed to be at work? It's nearly nine.
CAROLYN	Mom, I . . .
VAL	Carolyn, what's the matter? Are you sick?
CAROLYN	No. I'm taking the day off.
VAL	But you never take time off. Even when you broke your arm at recess you wouldn't go to emergency until school was over. *(anxious)* Honey, what's wrong?
CAROLYN	Mom, I have to talk to you.
VAL	*(fearful)* Okay.
CAROLYN	I need to tell you something.
VAL	*(steels herself)* Okay.

Tense pause.

CAROLYN	Mom, I'm a lesbian.
VAL	A what?
CAROLYN	A lesbian.
VAL	*(beat)* No, you're not. You were the prom queen! There was a stampede of boyfriends through this house for years. No way.
CAROLYN	I know it's a shock for you.
VAL	But you're not . . . one of those. You were always such a girlie girl, with the princess dresses and your doll collection . . .
CAROLYN	One in ten people is gay, Mom. And not all lesbians are stereotypical tomboys.
VAL	Now you're an expert?

CAROLYN	We learned about it in Women's Studies.
VAL	Is that where you got this idea? From your Women's Studies course? I paid for you to get talked into becoming a lesbian?!
CAROLYN	Come on, Mom, that makes no sense.
VAL	Neither does what you're telling me.
CAROLYN	I knew before I went away to university.
VAL	Well you could have fooled me. I wouldn't have bothered grounding you for being out with boys past your curfew if I'd known you didn't even like boys! *(beat)* You were never a lesbian!
CAROLYN	Remember when I went camping with Heather, from band? We sneaked a bottle of her parents' wine with us and drank it. And then we started kissing. That's when I first knew.
VAL	Heather? Little Heather from down the street?
CAROLYN	She's the same age as me, Mom.
VAL	Heather's engaged to be married. To a man!
CAROLYN	I know.
VAL	Carolyn, the thought of two women together disgusts me. I can't think about it. I feel sick.
CAROLYN	That's why I couldn't tell *you*.
VAL	But you told other people? And Keith? Does your brother know?
CAROLYN	Yes.
VAL	Everybody knew but me?
CAROLYN	Not everybody.
VAL	But most people. *(angry)* Why are you telling me this, now? Have you got a . . . what do you even call it? A "girlfriend" you want to invite for Christmas?
CAROLYN	Yes, I do. Her name's Sarah, but that's not—
VAL	I cannot live with that under my roof. You are

always welcome here but I cannot invite her. This isn't Toronto. Carolyn, I can't talk to you about this anymore.

CAROLYN   Mom . . .

VAL   Please just get the science kit and go.

CAROLYN retrieves the newspaper from its hiding place and gives it to VAL.

CAROLYN   It sometimes takes a family two or three or even five years. It can take a long time to accept. But I'm the same person I've always been. I haven't changed. Here's your paper.

CAROLYN exits to the bedroom. VAL sits down with the newspaper, in a daze.

VAL   *(to herself)* I can't live for two or three or five years without my daughter.

Distractedly, VAL unrolls her newspaper, reads the headline, and spills her coffee onto the paper. CAROLYN enters from the bedroom.

Oh my Lord.

CAROLYN   Did you read it?

VAL   You didn't take the day off.

CAROLYN   No.

VAL   But the kids love you, the parents love you . . . *(gesturing towards the newspaper)* I can't take all this in. What happened?

CAROLYN   Last weekend Sarah and I were at the Pride concert in Toronto. One of my grade fours, Kyle, was there with his mom, who turns out to be gay. On Monday he told me at recess that he saw me there.

VAL gasps.

I wasn't going to lie to him so I said, "yes." After recess the classroom was buzzing and Julia— always the ringleader—put up her hand and asked, "Are you gay?" I asked the class what being gay meant to them and Sam said, "It's two women who love each other or two men who love each other." *(beat)* I thought: if I lie about this when asked a direct question, what message does that send to students who feel different for *whatever* reason? The message would be that different is bad.

VAL   What happened?

CAROLYN   When Julia asked me "Are you gay?" I said, "yes." They all applauded and asked if they could come to the wedding.

VAL   The what?!

CAROLYN   We're not planning a wedding. They're in grade four, love and marriage go hand-in-hand for them. *(beat)* Most of the parents were very supportive, but a couple of them weren't.

VAL   Were you fired?

CAROLYN   They won't let me back into the classroom and I have a meeting with the teacher's union this morning. The union agrees that I'm in the right.

VAL   You're a wonderful teacher, Carolyn!

CAROLYN   I didn't want to make the same mistake with my students that I made with you. Hiding the truth. I should have told you long before today, instead you get a double shock.

VAL   Your sex life has nothing to do with what kind of teacher you are.

CAROLYN   I know. It doesn't affect the kind of daughter I am, either.

Pause.

VAL   It's so hard for me to understand because I would never, ever make that choice.

CAROLYN   What choice?

VAL   To be a lesbian.

CAROLYN   It's not a choice, Mom. It's who I am. I can choose to tell you or not tell you, but I can't change who I am.

VAL   You're my daughter, Carolyn. I'll always love you.

They embrace.

           Tell me about . . .

CAROLYN   Sarah.

VAL   Tell me about Sarah.

CAROLYN   You'd really like her, Mom. She has a great sense of humour and she loves to cook. She's a vet in Toronto. *(beat)* There's only one thing.

VAL   What?

CAROLYN   She has a St. Bernard and a black Lab.

VAL   Dogs. The final frontier.

END

Troupe
by Ron Fromstein

Four women attend the one hundred and tenth meeting of the Khodoriv Dance Collective.

Troupe premiered at Toronto Cold Reads.

CHARACTER LIST

Martina	A leader of sorts
Helga	A dancer to the end
Natalya	A talker
Tessa	The group diplomat

SETTING

A small village in the Ukraine.

...

Ron Fromstein is a Toronto-born and -based playwright/writer. He is a multiple winner and finalist of the Canadian National Playwriting Competition. Works include *The Big Smoke*, *Dianne & Me*, *Zach Zultana*, and *One in a Million* (a micromusical).

Troupe

A converted dance studio.

That is, there is dance equipment but also bookshelves, children's drawings on the wall, easels in the corners, etc.

Centre. Several chairs.

A few women sit.

One knits. This is TESSA.

One sits, observant. This is MARTINA.

One stretches and/or dances. This is HELGA.

MARTINA	Helga:
HELGA	Yes.
MARTINA	Please.
HELGA	I am sorry she is dead. I am. I am sorry rehearsal went late and there was a bear there after. Like it was waiting. Who would have thought it? But what can you do?
MARTINA	We can sit like human beings. Mourn.

HELGA	We are dancers, Martina.
TESSA	Ida was a good dancer.
HELGA	My point exactly.
TESSA	Maybe we should sit.
MARTINA	Yes.
TESSA	And then after, who knows.
MARTINA	It is like you are stepping on her grave.
HELGA	I am not stepping on anyone.
MARTINA	I said it is like.
TESSA	Now, now.
MARTINA	Tessa.
TESSA	What—I can't speak.
HELGA	Let her talk.
TESSA	Thank you. I understand your dancing. I do. It is good to dance.
HELGA	Yes, it is.
TESSA	And I understand your reluctance to do as Helga does.
MARTINA	You do.
TESSA	I do. I think. I hope.
MARTINA	Good. *(loud)* Natalya!

A woman comes in on the phone.

This is NATALYA.

NATALYA	*(into phone)* —You're sure it is the same everywhere. I don't know. Maybe there are parts where it is one way and other parts where it is another. Maybe—
MARTINA	We need you.
NATALYA	*(quiet)* —Ivan has caught no fish today.
TESSA	How is Ivan?

MARTINA	Tessa!
NATALYA	*(into phone)* —No, I'm not telling them. I just said—I. Ivan, please.
TESSA	*(quiet)* —It is a difficult job.
MARTINA	*(in kind)* —In particular with a dead river.
NATALYA	It is not dead. It is not! *(to phone)* Ivan—hi. It was about something else? About what? . . . about a dance we no longer do. I should save some minutes for later. Yes, I would like it if you picked me up later. Don't forget the rifle. *(to everyone)* I am here.
TESSA	Good to have you.
MARTINA	Helga.
HELGA	Yes.
MARTINA	Can we talk now?
HELGA	Please do.
MARTINA	Can you please . . .
HELGA	You are as you are, I am as I am.
TESSA	I like that. As you are. As we are. I like that. *(to MARTINA)* What?
MARTINA	Fine. Now commencing the . . .
TESSA	One hundred and tenth.
MARTINA	One hundred and tenth meeting of the Khodoriv Dance Collective. All present.
TESSA	Present.
NATALYA	Here.
MARTINA	Helga.
HELGA	You know I am here.
TESSA	You're supposed to say it.
HELGA	Here. Present.
TESSA	Thank you.

MARTINA	We mourn the passing of sister Ida and now must consider how to move forward. Secretary:
TESSA	That's me.
MARTINA	And . . .
TESSA	It is as you said. I have checked. No one wants to join at the moment. No one young. No one old.
MARTINA	Thank you. We have a number of options. Helga thinks we should just keep on as we were.
NATALYA	I agree . . .
MARTINA	What are you doing?
NATALYA	I think the same.
TESSA	The chair didn't ask for comments yet.
NATALYA	Oh.
TESSA	May I.
MARTINA	You may.
TESSA	The chair and the secretary will now take comments.
NATALYA	Good. I say—dance while you can dance. Fish while you can fish.
MARTINA	Only now there are no more fish.
TESSA	Martina.
NATALYA	That's all right. All the more reason to then. All the more reason to move while you can. Leap while you can. Catch and be caught.

And now two are dancing.

MARTINA	Natalya, Helga.
TESSA	Maybe we could say a prayer.
MARTINA	That would be nice, yes.
TESSA	Helga and Natalya?
NATALYA	Yes.
HELGA	Sure.

TESSA	You were a good dancer, Ida. A good friend.
MARTINA	Yes, she was.
NATALYA	Very much so.
HELGA	Yes.

And now TESSA *rises.*

And begins dancing.

MARTINA	Tessa.
TESSA	Yes.
MARTINA	What are you doing.
TESSA	We said a prayer, yes.
MARTINA	We did, yes.
TESSA	And so . . .
MARTINA	So:
HELGA	Who believes we should keep on as we were?
NATALYA	I.
MARTINA	Tessa.
TESSA	Sorry. I.
HELGA	I. And there it is. Tessa.
TESSA	Yes.
NATALYA	A vote has been made.
TESSA	So it has. Martina:
MARTINA	Yes, Tessa.
TESSA	A vote has been made.
MARTINA	Yes.
TESSA	And passed.
MARTINA	I heard.
TESSA	And so . . .
MARTINA	Okay. Okay.

MARTINA *rises and dances reluctantly.*

TESSA   Thank you very much, Martina, for—

MARTINA   Tessa.

TESSA   Yes.

MARTINA   Please don't talk just now.

And TESSA *nods.*

All dance.

Lights.

Brother, Brother
A short play
by Meghan Greeley

A little girl with a speech impediment must learn to pronounce five important words by tomorrow. She's found someone to help, but his unorthodox method is going to cost her.

Brother, Brother premiered at the InspiraTO Festival in Toronto, Ontario, directed by Dale Sheldrake and with projections designed by Lumir Hladik, featuring Danny Parkes (as Boy) and Madeleine Brown (as Girl).

CHARACTER LIST

Boy   (a teenager)
Girl   (a young child)

SETTING

An empty urban schoolyard. Late afternoon.

...

Meghan Greeley is a writer and performer. Originally from Newfoundland, she currently resides in Toronto where she is a member of the Tarragon Theatre Playwrights Unit and an MFA candidate in Screenwriting at York University. She holds a BFA in Theatre (Acting) from Memorial University.

Meghan's stage play *Kingdom* was produced by White Rooster Theatre in St. John's (2012) and later toured to the Stages Theatre Festival in Halifax (2013). It was then produced by Contra Theatre at the Tarragon Theatre Workspace (2016). *Kingdom* is published in *The Breakwater Book of Contemporary Newfoundland Plays, Volume 1*.

White Rooster produced her full-length play *Hunger* in November 2015. The script was nominated for the RBC Tarragon Emerging Playwright Prize.

Brother, Brother, originally commissioned by Engine Productions for its Queer Theatre Festival's Short and Queer Show, was a winner of the 2015 InspiraTO Festival's short play contest and was produced at the Alumnae Theatre in Toronto. Other awards include: RCA Statoil Young Playwriting Series (2010), the Magnetic North Under 25 Playwriting Contest (2006), and the Sparks Literary Festival's Poetry Competition (2015).

Brother, Brother

Darkness. The sounds of a shrill school bell and then a chain-link fence rattling in the wind. Lights rise on a BOY, *centre stage. Thrown to one side is a backpack. He is gazing outward. Focused. He lifts a hand and, with a gesture, begins to mime that he is holding a basketball. He lifts the other hand and begins to toss this invisible ball back and forth between them. He bounces the ball, eyes straight ahead—presumably, in the space that the audience occupies, there is a basketball net. The* BOY *poises himself to shoot. With a flick of his wrists he sends the invisible ball sailing into the air. He watches its supposed flight path.*

BOY   Oh, man.

Evidently, he has missed. He mimes the retrieval of the ball. A young GIRL, *dressed in baggy boy's clothing and wearing a baseball cap, enters. She watches in silence as he mimes another shot for the basket. This time, upon retrieving the invisible ball, he notices her.*

          Let me see it.

The GIRL *reaches into the pockets of her jacket and removes two fistfuls of change.*

How much is that?

The GIRL dumps the coins on the ground and holds up four fingers. The BOY tucks the invisible basketball under one arm.

I told you five. Five dollars, five words.

She looks down. Nudges a coin with her sneaker.

Hey. Catch.

The BOY mimes tossing the invisible ball to her. She doesn't move.

What are you doing? You were supposed to catch it. Are you going to just let it roll away?

The GIRL looks around, confused.

GIRL   But . . . but it's . . .

BOY   What, you don't see it?

The GIRL shakes her head.

That's cause it's invisible.

The GIRL opens her mouth to speak. Changes her mind.

Well? Go get it.

The GIRL looks around. She looks to the BOY for affirmation before walking a few steps.

What are you doing? It's over there.

He points her in the opposite direction. She obeys. She stoops and mimes picking up the invisible ball. Unconvincingly, she tosses it back in the BOY's direction. He mimes stopping it with one foot.

All right. Four dollars, four words. We compromise. You know that word? Com-pro-mise?

She nods. The BOY retrieves his backpack, begins to unzip it.

Sit.

She sits. The BOY takes a piece of chalk out of his bag. He rolls it towards her.

Write them down.

The GIRL takes the chalk and begins to write on the ground. The BOY removes a knife from his backpack. Then a fork. Then a plate. He sets these on the ground as though preparing for a crude picnic. Then he takes a bar of soap from his bag and puts it on the plate. He stands and looks over her shoulder. She has written the words—

Brother, truck, remember, roll. Okay.

The BOY resumes a sitting position opposite her.

Ready?

She nods.

Repeat after me. *(over-enunciating)* Bro-therrr.

The GIRL hesitates. When she speaks, it is with a soft impediment; she can't pronounce the letter R.

GIRL   Bwu-tha.

BOY   Nope. That's wrong. Take a bite.

She looks from the soap to the BOY.

Trust me. It's gonna cure you.

She takes the soap in her hands, lifts it to her mouth. He grabs it from her.

Hey, we aren't savages. Use your knife and fork.

He sets the soap back on the plate. She lifts the utensils and tries to cut it like a steak. She gets a piece on the fork and lifts it to her mouth.

Make sure you chew before you swallow. That's important.

The GIRL chews. She swallows and gags.

Gross, huh?

She nods.

What did I tell you earlier?

GIRL   That . . . that . . .

BOY   That it wouldn't be easy. That's the point. You're teaching yourself a lesson. Know how I know?

She shakes her head.

Because it worked for me.

GIRL   It did?

BOY   Absolutely. Worked like a miracle. Doctors don't even know about the secret cure.

She nods with wonder.

Let's try again. Bro-therrr.

GIRL   B . . . bwu-tha.

He shakes his head. Taps her plate. She lifts another piece of soap to her mouth.

BOY   Let's try the next one. Trrr-uck.

GIRL   Twu—twu—twuck.

BOY   Wrong. Re-mem-berrr.

GIRL   Wemembeh.

BOY   Wrong. Rrrr-oll.

GIRL   Woll.

BOY   That's three wrong. That means three bites.

She puts another piece in her mouth.

Come on. Just make the sound. Arrrrr.

GIRL   Ahhh.

BOY   More like a pirate. Arrrrrrrrr.

GIRL   Ahhhhhhh.

BOY   Not even close. Do you want to try some other words?

She shakes her head.

Why not? We could try, uh—hey! Pirate. Or princess, maybe. Don't you want to learn how to say princess?

GIRL   I can't. I need to luhn these wohds foh my speech
                        tomowoh.

BOY   Speech—tomorrow? Is that what you said? You're
                        gonna make a speech?

She nods.

GIRL   You said you would help me. I gave you foh
                        dollehs.

BOY   Fine. Read me your speech.

GIRL   You teach me to say it wight?

BOY   Four dollars worth of right.

*She removes a crumpled piece of paper from her pocket. She
smooths it lovingly with her hands. This is clearly something of
value. She looks at the BOY, awaiting his signal.*

                        Go ahead.

GIRL   *(reading)* I will miss my big bwutha. I am so sad
                        that he got hit by a twuck and died. I will always
                        wemembeh how he taught me to woll my tongue.
                        I will miss him fo—ffff—

She falters. Silence.

BOY   The fifth word . . . is it forever?

She nods. Silence.

GIRL   That's my speech.

BOY   That's called a eulogy.

GIRL   Will you teach me to say it wight?

BOY   I can't.

*The GIRL removes her baseball cap. She begins to drop the coins
into it. He watches her, suddenly uncomfortable.*

                        Look—are you a boy or a girl, anyway?

The GIRL lifts the chalk. She writes the word girl *on the ground.*

                        Then why don't you dress like one?

She circles the letter R *in* girl. *It takes him a moment to understand, but then he does.*

There's no *R* in *boy.*

GIRL   Yeah. But you know what?

BOY   What?

GIRL   Soon I'll be a woman.

Beat. The BOY *puts the utensils and soap back in his bag. The* GIRL *stands to go.*

BOY   Hey . . . you want to learn how to play ball?

GIRL   I need to go home and pwactice my eulogy. So I can say it wight.

BOY   It was right.

He stands. Mimes picking up the invisible ball.

Ready?

GIRL   But it isn't . . .

BOY   Real?

She nods.

Come on. Stand beside me over here.

She stands. He mimes putting the ball in her hands. She accepts.

Got it?

GIRL   Got it.

BOY   Careful, don't drop it. Keep your eyes on the net up there. Make sure you line it up. Now, when you're ready, take a deep breath . . .

She takes a deep breath.

. . . and throw the ball.

She throws. They both watch the ball's imaginary flight path. She turns to the BOY.

GIRL   Did it go in?

He mimes the retrieval of the ball.

BOY   Man . . . nice one. I never get it on the first try.

He tosses it back to her. She catches it. Smiles.

Blackout.

It's Going to Be a Bright
by Matthew Heiti

Two people break up and then break apart. And then break again.
And again.

It's Going to Be a Bright was commissioned by Productions Roches
brûlées for Nearly Urban Stories, an evening of monologues, performed at the Art Gallery of Sudbury in February 2014. Special
thanks to Miriam Cusson.

CHARACTER LIST

Waiter

···

Born in a meteor crater called Sudbury, Matthew Heiti holds an MA in Creative Writing from the University of New Brunswick. He is an award-winning playwright, a Genie-nominated screenwriter, and his first novel, *The City Still Breathing*, is published by Coach House Books. His play about teen mental health, *Black Dog: 4 vs the wrld*, is published by Playwrights Canada Press. Matthew currently serves as Playwright-in-Residence with Pat the Dog Theatre Creation, where he is co-director of PlaySmelter, Northern Ontario's first workshop and reading festival of new plays. With the Sudbury Theatre Centre, he has run the Playwrights' Junction, a workshop for developing writers. In his downtime, he works on old bicycles and explores new work in abandoned places with Crestfallen. Some of his writing can be found at www.harkback.org.

It's Going to Be a Bright

A person, perhaps a WAITER, *in squeaky-clean clothes, perfectly manicured. Clinical.*

A table. Two empty chairs facing each other. Two plates, utensils, wine glasses—lipstick on one. A covered silver serving tray in the middle. An art exhibit, a crime scene.

The WAITER *stands behind the table, between the two settings. A presentation.*

They lift the lid of the tray with a flourish. A turntable, a record on it. They lift the arm and set it spinning.

WAITER

Beep beep. Beep beep—7:41 a.m.—Beep beep. Beep beep—wakey wakey eggs and bakey—Beep beep. Beep beep—they throw the covers off and they throw the record on the turntable—lift the arm, set the needle spinning—shit shower shave—spinning—black coffee, dry toast—spinning—shirts skirts slacks—spinning—out the door, down the street—spinning—to work, break, work, lunch, work, break, work—up the street, in the door—spinning.

Spinning today like every day, the same spinning, to the same record.

Only where they used to spin together, they now spin separately. I can . . . see . . .

> *Snaps to attention.*

I can see—

I can see—

I can see—

Nothing to break the mundane day-to-day dallying through the doldrums, desperate for any discrepancy, disturbance, difference in the day-to-day, the day-to-day, daily decreasing, dimly depressing, deadly deceasing.

> *Relaxes. Invites us in.*

They meet at the art gallery. They look at the paintings. "Nice," he says. "Yes," she says, "nice." Nice being a nice inoffensive word to use because they're both nice people now.

They go for dinner, the first time in twelve months and they are seated at the same table they always used to sit at, both laughing—ha ha, ho ho—that it should be the same table.

She's eating veal again, always ordering it like it should be a surprise, something dangerous or twisted she's doing, before her first bite with the meat dripping on the fork, saying, "I just feel so guilty." Never mind there are so many bites of veal in her past she should be a Hindenburg of guilt by now. She leaves one little piece of pinkish meat near the edge of her plate like an apology, like a statement: "I just couldn't finish it."

He orders something different, as if to say, "I'm impulsive, and adventurous, I'm a new man, I'm better." Right away he wishes he'd just ordered the same thing he always did. They both know he's no better, no worse, just the same. Like a record. Spinning. The record. The record. He's chicken parm, side salad, balsamic vinaigrette. The record. The record.

The food hurts his belly. Heartburn? Indigestion? No.

They have wine. He's white, she's . . . red.

"She always drank white, why's she drinking red?"

"She never liked white, she only drank so that he wouldn't feel like such a loser drinking white wine alone."

"Oh. How's that friend of hers?"

"Audrey? Still fighting with her boyfriend."

"What a prick."

"Yeah, what a prick." A brief moment of camaraderie, she continues— "How are his parents?"

"Good. Except his mother died."

"Oh yeah, she's sorry for not going to the funeral, but it wouldn't have been, you know, appropriate."

"Yeah."

"Yeah."

"Yeah."

"So."

"So."

"Yeah."

"So."

"Yeah."

"So."

"So."

"Yeah."

"So."

"So."

And so on. They order dessert. Both cheesecake. Turtle?

"No."

White chocolate?

"No."

Raspberry?

"No. Don't you have plain cheesecake? No frills, nothing decadent, just cheesecake. The same cheesecake they always ordered. The same cheesecake." The record. The record.

New York–style.

They each get their own. The cake hurts his stomach. Lactose intolerance? Impacted bowel? Dysentery? No.

"Remember when they used to share? She loved sharing."

"Yeah, so she says, but she always ate more than half."

"He's just being petty."

"No, he's just joking."

"Well, he's not funny."

"She always used to call him petty, but he wasn't petty, he was just precise."

"Well, he's precisely being an asshole."

They don't share, but they each precisely leave one half of their cake. Plates are cleared. One bill or two?

"One."

"Two."

"Two."

Separate. Once one now two. Two bills sliced precisely in half like the two pieces of leftover cake. Bills paid separately. She tips well, he tips . . . well, he doesn't.

Do they want to take home the leftovers?

"No."

"No, thanks."

Neither of them wants anything to remember this by. Anyway, he can't eat anything what with this pain in his stomach, worse now today than the day before. Gastritis? No. Liver failure? No. Something worse. Something much worse.

Conversation all puckered up like a pair of old lips. Nothing left to say. Except—

"Well."

"Well."

"Well."

"Well."

"Well."

"Well."

Well, well, well. Well, it goes on like this for a while. Asses superglued to seats by some messy recipe of guilt, obligation, nostalgia, and indifference. They make sure not to mention the names of the new penises and vaginas with which they keep company most recently.

Fast-forward to the parking lot. "Do you want a ride?" she says.

"No. I like walking."

"It's raining."

"I like walking."

"And you don't have an umbrella."

"I like walking." She never listened to him.

"He was always such a martyr," she thinks but she says, "Come to the car. I have a box of your stuff you never picked up."

Oh, the inevitable swap meet of abandoned and orphaned detritus. Like trenches of the dead left behind by warring armies. Single socks and old VHS tapes, random kitchen utensils and photographs of the two of them together looking vaguely joyful. Things that neither of them want to lay claim to.

An awkward moment with the rain coming down and the trunk open. "Should she hug him?" she thinks. "Should they shake hands?"

"Is she going to kiss him?" he wonders. "Does he want her to? Would it be more victorious to let her kiss him or to stop her?"

"Why is his mouth hanging open like that?"

She shuts the trunk with a symbolic slam and they sit on the bumper.

"What happened to the old Saturn?" he says. "I loved that car."

"I hated it. I traded it in."

"For an SUV. That's so suburban of you."

"It's safer for kids."

"But you don't have any kids. You don't even have the stickers on your rear windshield to prove it." He laughs at his own stupid joke. She's not laughing.

"I have some news." she says. She says it in slow motion, driving in each word like a dagger.

I—stab—Have—stab—Some—stab—News. Stab stab.

News is new, it's not old. News is not the same. Chicken parm, side salad, balsamic vinaigrette. The record. The record.

He can't hear her. He's spinning—Beep beep—the alarm that morning—Beep beep 7:41 a.m.—but no record on the turntable. The same record they used to spin every morning before work is missing. Where is it? Did he lose it? I can see . . .

> *Snap.*

I can see—

I can see—

I can see—

He's got some news too. He wants to tell her, "My belly. Me too. I'm making something too. I'm doing something too. I'm growing too."

She remembers all their talk in bed, listening to that record. The record. The record. Room colours, crib wood, baby names. The record. The record.

Played so much the needle's diamond-drilled the grooves into vinyl canyons. Spinning and finally skipping. Skipping. The record. The record. Stuck on "I can see"—the record—I can see clearly now—the record—the rain, the table, the chicken parm—the record—slam the trunk—I've got news.

Home again, home again, jiggety-jig. Invert, pervert the morning routine. Stuff that goes on comes off. He rewinds himself under the sheets. He sleeps.

Beep beep. Beep beep—the pain wakes him—Beep beep. Beep beep—something's wrong, it's 3:22 a.m.—Beep beep goes his belly—

Beep beep. It's time, but it's too early. It's not nine months yet, not even 7:41 a.m. He runs to the washroom. Ring ring. Answers the phone on the toilet. Ring Ring. She's crying. Blood blood. On the sheets. Blood blood. Crying. Blood blood.

He says, "Me too."

A universe of his insides in the toilet. Flush.

Spinning, red spinning down her bowl. Flush.

The record. The record.

He paces the house. Round and round. Spinning. Wearing a groove into the carpet. And he finds it here by the door. The box of his things from her trunk. Digging through to the bottom to find a package wrapped in paper. Tearing off the paper to find a record. Just one. The record. THE record. Johnny Nash's smiling face. Pulling out the paper sleeve. The record. THE record.

> *They take the record off the turntable. Pulls it into their belly. Winding tighter and tighter.*

I can see—

The record.

The record.

I can see—

The record.

The record.

I can see—

The rec

The rec

I can see—

The rec

The rec

I can see—

A crack. They open their arms. Blood covering their belly. The record in two neat halves.

The wreck.

The wreck.

Oh, the wreck.

They place one half on each of the plates.

END

Garbed in Flesh
A verse play in ten minutes
by Arthur Holden

Confronted by a youthful detective, and then by his own outraged wife, an aging sexual predator reveals himself to be more than he seems . . . and less than he claims to be.

CHARACTER LIST

Detective (F)   thirties, she's wearing business attire
Man (M)   sixties, he's clad in ragged clothes
Hera (F)   sixties, she wears a long Grecian gown

SETTING

An interrogation room.
A table. Two chairs. On the floor, in a corner, a maimed child's doll.
Upstage, a raised platform.

...

Arthur Holden's plays have been presented in Montreal, Calgary, New York, and London. He lives in Montreal with novelist Claire Holden Rothman. They have two grown sons.

Garbed in Flesh

Lights up.

The MAN *is sitting on a chair, his wrists manacled to the table.*

The DETECTIVE *enters.*

DETECTIVE   How are you feeling? Are the cuffs too tight?
              Perhaps you'd like a soda or a bite
              to eat. You don't look very well. Feel free
              to ask for anything you need. I'll see
              to it that, within reason, your request
              is granted.

MAN   I want you to get undressed.
              To straddle me. I want to hear your sighs,
              I want to feel the quaking of your thighs
              as I press deep, then deeper, hard and true,
              into the hot wet trembling core of you,
              until my fire-white seed flies in an arc
              and fills your belly, and the world goes dark.

DETECTIVE   Excuse me?

MAN   Choose to be my chosen one,
              and when I'm finished, when the deed is done,

draw solace in your drab declining days
from knowing you lay briefly in the gaze
of immortality. You touched a god.

DETECTIVE   Ah. Right. The age-old ploy. Pretend you're odd.
You think it profits you to play the fool.
You think the system won't be quite so cruel
if I'm persuaded that you've lost your mind.
Sorry. You're not that smart. I'm not that kind.
So you can cut the crap. I'm here for facts.
I want a full recital of your acts
from start to finish. It's time to confess.
But first things first: your name, age, and address.

MAN   I have a multitude of names: great Jove;
stern Jupiter, lord of the timeless grove;
stupendous Zeus, ruler of night and day.
All creatures move and breathe under my sway.

DETECTIVE   Perhaps my explanation wasn't clear.
You have nothing to gain and much to fear
from this display of feigned insanity.
If you persist, if you keep baiting me,
I'll have you thrown into the holding cell
downstairs, and you'll find out first-hand what hell
is like. You've had your fun. You've played your games.
You've called yourself a string of silly names.
But now all that is going to stop. Take care
what you say next. Don't push your luck. I swear,
if I hear even one more little lie,
I'll toss you in that cell, and you will die
an awful death inflicted by a pack
of men who, when they learn of your attack,
won't pity your false madness or true age.
They will bear down on you in righteous rage.
You see, molesters don't do well in jail.
They're viewed as monsters, they're beyond the pale.
When jailhouse justice comes, it isn't swift
or merciful. You will beg for the gift
of death, which will be brutally delayed
until disfigured, mutilated, flayed,

you finally croak. Now, I don't give a shit
what name you call yourself. Zeus? So be it.
But there's a teenaged girl, battered, confused,
who, hours ago, was viciously abused.
She's traumatized, raving about a bird,
a man in ragged clothes. Her speech is slurred,
her body's bruised and bloody. She was raped.
Patrolmen found you snoring, mouth agape,
at dawn behind the boathouse in the park,
right where the girl says she was jumped as dark
was falling. I'm sure you can understand
why I've concluded you're that ragged man.

MAN   I am no man. I am a deity.

DETECTIVE   Don't go there, dirtbag. Don't you fuck with me.
I want to know what happened to the girl.

MAN   You dare address the master of the world
with brazen insolence? Prepare to die.
My thunderbolts will pierce the panicked sky.
They'll bake your bones in a titanic flash;
and in three seconds, you'll be smoke and ash.

*The MAN tugs at his manacles. He tries to stand up, but can't.
He sinks back onto the chair.*

DETECTIVE   I'm waiting. One . . . two . . . three . . . oops. Still
alive.
Do you need three more seconds? Maybe five?
Or will you give up on your sad charade?
Admit defeat. The shoddy tricks you played
were all for nothing.

MAN   Suddenly I'm tired.

DETECTIVE   Of course you are. Unnatural desire
takes effort. You're a long way from your youth.
Now tell me what you did. I want the truth.

MAN   The truth . . . the truth . . . oh, Hera, slide, glide
down.
I know the things I've done have made you frown.
Dear wife of mine, indulge me, lift me up.
Come rescue me, and I will put the cup
away from these dry lips. I will abstain . . .

DETECTIVE   Do you have any notion of the pain
you'll face inside that holding cell? Those guys
will cut your gonads off. They'll gouge the eyes
out of your head and shove them up your ass.
They'll decorate your throat with shards of glass.
I'm out of patience, and you're out of time.
You're down to one last chance. Confess your
crime . . .

HERA *appears on the upstage platform.*

[Note: it should be apparent that HERA *is visible to the* MAN *but
not to the* DETECTIVE.*]*

HERA   Enough. This is demeaning.

DETECTIVE   Wait . . . what . . . who . . .?

HERA   You could have done
the things I told you to.
For once, you could have listened when I talked.
But no. Ever the slave to your own cock.

DETECTIVE   Who are you? Show yourself!

HERA   I am his wife.

MAN   And harshest critic. Let's postpone the strife
till later, shall we? I just want to leave
this place. I'm ready for a long reprieve
from skin and bone.

DETECTIVE   Are you outside the door?

The DETECTIVE *hurries offstage. After a moment she comes
back, having obviously found no one.*

Meanwhile the exchange between HERA *and the* MAN *continues . . .*

HERA   Who was she?

MAN   Someone I'd not seen before.
She'll never know a man to equal me.

HERA   Where is your honour? Where's your dignity?
You've done appalling harm, yet feel no shame.
The time has come for you to take the blame,
acknowledge the extent of your offence.
To violate a child is so immense,

so sordid, so grotesque, so horrible,
it verges on the inconceivable.
Do not equivocate. Do not deny.
You will look this young woman in the eye.
You will confess your crime. You will atone.

MAN   I will do no such thing, you tiresome crone.
                 I . . .

HERA   Silence! Is it freedom that you seek?
                 Or is it torture in a jail cell? Speak.
                 Confess. And don't you dare attempt to lie:
                 for you are garbed in flesh, and flesh can die.

The MAN *composes himself. Quietly at first, but with increasing heat, he speaks to the* DETECTIVE.

MAN   The light is draining from the day. It's dusk.
                 I'm on a cloud. I catch a whiff of musk,
                 a soft sweet scent of blooming womanhood:
                 a girl whose first warm flush of female blood
                 has come just as she's entering the park
                 all by herself. There, in the gathering dark,
                 I see the budding breasts, the milky glide
                 of lithe young legs moving with rapid stride
                 beside the lake. A flood of white-hot lust
                 sweeps over me and, sudden as a gust
                 of wind, I am the swan in Leda's dream:
                 a man. A bird. A man. She tries to scream.
                 I pull her, muffled in my creamy plumes,
                 behind the boathouse. Loamy flowering fumes
                 rise thickly as I tear off underclothes.
                 A moment, an eternity . . . who knows
                 how long it lasts? I gasp. I am ablaze.
                 I am asleep. I wake up in a daze.
                 The girl is gone. Two burly, surly men
                 put flimsy chains around my wrists and then
                 transport me here inside a metal cart.
                 Next, you come in. I feel a tingle start
                 to warm my loins—but you turn insolent.
                 I call down lightning from the firmament.
                 I wait . . . and wait . . . and wait. No fiery spear
                 obliterates you. With a nasty sneer,

you mock the very thought that I'm a god.
You scorn me as a liar and a fraud.
I cannot break these thin pathetic chains.
I'm trapped inside this body. I'm in pain.

He turns to HERA.

What's happened to me, Hera? Where's my strength?
Where's the gigantic force that spanned the length
and breadth of all creation?

HERA
It is gone.
The world's no longer yours to prey upon.
The rules have changed.

MAN
But I'm not bound by rules.
Such things exist to torment slaves and fools.
I am the god who governs night and day.
All creatures move and breathe under my sway.
Who ever dared hold me accountable?
How many girls, young and desirable,
have lain, helpless with terror, in my power,
to scratch the random itch of half an hour?
I took Callisto and Antiope,
Aegina, Io, timid Semele,
Europa, Maera . . .

HERA
Yes. The list is long.
And each assault was a prodigious wrong.
A woman's body is her own to share
or to preserve, always and everywhere.
A girl too young to grant informed consent
must not be touched. The gravest punishment
is meted out to those who dare infringe
these principles. There must be harsh revenge
when innocence is shattered. This I know.
Unbending justice has decreed it so.

MAN
Your words apply to mortals, not to me.

HERA
True justice is for all. Thus shall it be
from now until the star-filled dome grows dim.

MAN
This perfect blooming nymph, so young and slim,
entices me: she drives my senses wild
as she drifts, half a woman, half a child,
into the park. She robs me of repose . . .
and *I'm* to blame? Do you reproach the rose
for fragrance? This is what I am. The earth
and all its transient things are only worth
the momentary value of desire.
I have no guilt. My freedom is entire.

HERA
Your freedom's partial and contingent . . .

MAN
                                                                    Wrong!
Don't try to limit me. I don't belong
among these crawling, rule-bound little folk.
Your principles, the ones you claim I broke,
do not apply. I'm utterly exempt.

HERA
In days to come, if some young woman tempts
you . . .

MAN
                                    I will swoop down. I will scoop her up.

HERA
You promised me that you would put the cup
away from those dry lips: that you'd abstain.

MAN
A god says many things when he's in pain.

HERA
You lied?

MAN
                                    Of course. Now get me out of here.

HERA
I'll set you free another way, poor dear.

MAN
What does that mean?

HERA
                                                            You should have stayed on
high.
On earth, you're garbed in flesh. And flesh can
die.

HERA extends one arm in the MAN's direction. He gasps and clutches his chest.

The DETECTIVE rushes over and tries to help him. In vain. The MAN slumps forward.

The DETECTIVE takes his pulse. She looks around wildly, addressing HERA—whom she still can't see.

DETECTIVE	What have you done? No breath, no pulse . . . he's dead.
HERA	What choice had I? You heard the things he said. He couldn't shed his blind destructiveness. Should I have left him to the wantonness of blood-crazed inmates: I, his loyal wife, the friend and adversary of his life? It's fitting that the end should come through me. I too am a stupendous deity.
DETECTIVE	But I'm a human being, a lowly cop guarding a man whose death I didn't stop and can't explain. The brass will want to know: how did I end up with a stiff John Doe? Oh, Hera—if that's who you are, and not some dream assailing overloaded thoughts— please, don't forsake me. I need sound advice.
HERA	Describe what happened. Don't be too precise. Just say the suspect in your custody was plainly in poor health, and suddenly his heart failed: all of which is strictly true, though it omits a small detail or two. Somehow I doubt your senior officers lose sleep over the death of predators.
DETECTIVE	And you . . . you've lost your monarch. Jupiter is gone. Who will stand in as arbiter and lawgiver?
HERA	I have someone in mind: a certain goddess, sensible and kind, whose long experience of gross misrule has taught her to control her temper, cool her passions, and strive always to do right. Imagine that: the gods, with radiant light, behaving decently in ages hence, worthy, at last, of their magnificence. It's time to go. We both have much to do. May Fate in her great wisdom smile on you.

HERA *disappears.*

The DETECTIVE *contemplates the* MAN.

DETECTIVE   All creatures moved and breathed under your sway.
Look at you now. Stillness. Silence. Decay.
The page has turned. I'll try to help that girl;
and, step by tiny step, perhaps we can improve the world.

She goes to the maimed doll on the floor and takes it tenderly in her arms. Then she exits.

The MAN's *lifeless body just sits there.*

Lights out.

THE END

A *Recipe for Tomato Butter*
by Florence Gibson MacDonald

Maeve, a sixty-one-year-old woman contemplating God, tomatoes, and September 11, reaches across the fence to her neighbours, a Middle Eastern woman and her kids.

A *Recipe for Tomato Butter* was commissioned by CBC Radio for the first anniversary of September 11. Starring Rosemary Dunsmore, produced and directed by James Roy, it aired on the program *Loss and Legacy*.

CHARACTER LIST

Maeve

...

Florence Gibson MacDonald has written several award-winning plays, including the internationally produced *Belle*, as well as *Elevator, Take Care of Me, Home is My Road, Missing,* and *How Do I Love Thee?* With choreographer Shawn Byfield she co-created the Dora Award–winning tap dance show, *i think i can*. She is currently working on her one-woman show *Love Handles* and her novel *Stout*.

A Recipe for Tomato Butter

MAEVE, *sixty-one, at her house, a semi-detached in downtown Toronto.*

MAEVE

I let the cable go when I turned fifty-nine, and Bud died, and I suppose you could say it's all been downhill from there.

"You're letting yourself go, Mom," Sheila said when she made a flying visit from Vancouver and I'd no idea we had a new mayor. Because I'd also stopped the paper three months before, I mean, what was the point? It seemed to me no news was good news.

So when my brother-in-law phoned from Cornwall to tell me the planes had hit the Trade towers and another one aimed at the Pentagon—he's Bud's brother, and he still looks out for me—I guess he figured, out here in the wilds of downtown Toronto, if worse came to worst, I wouldn't know when to duck.

As it was I could have missed the call altogether. I was out in the backyard, looking at the tomatoes. That first spring without Bud I didn't put any in at all, and this spring Tiffany comes with plants—on orders from Sheila it turns out—and says "we're missing the tomato butter, Mom." And now it's September 11 and they're rotting on the vine so all hopes of making it are going up in smoke, when she comes out. I call her "she" because she doesn't speak English so we don't converse, just nod and smile a lot, two women across a backyard fence. We're joined at the hip to their semi-detached—a rental, landlord's decent, a Maltese I'm told—so when their phone rings I think it's mine. It's usually hers, they've been here about a year and a half, she gets a lot of calls from relatives overseas. But this time she comes out telegraphing to me through our usual sign languages that it's my phone.

Well at first I think it's a joke. So I turn on the CBC Radio. And then I round up my daughters. Kind of hard to do with Sheila out in Vancouver trying to break into film and our Tiffany in Oakville passing herself off as married.

But we talk, and make sure each of us is all right. Tiffany crying and Sheila mad as a hornet, the usual from each of them, same when their dad died, same for everything. Sheila blames men and Tiff blames herself.

I took them to a pro-choice rally when they were little and I think that's when they got set in cement, their attitudes. I took them because Dad was a doctor who looked after the "woman problem" when it was illegal so I knew all the stories, growing up. Now Sheila's got herself all involved, sports this T-shirt with a picture of the Nativity and one of the wise "persons" proclaiming, "It's a girl!" Says she gets a lot of comments. Sparks a lot of discussion amongst her crowd.

Anyway, I get the news about the world coming to an end and I thank Bruce very much and I hang up the phone and go back outside to stare at the tomatoes.

Because the bottom line is I don't care. About the planes or the tomatoes or religion or anything. Sheila was right about letting myself go. I'm a virtual deserter.

Then she comes out. Tears streaming down her face. And I gather from the way she looks up at the sky that it's the planes that's upset her. And she's got all her kids crying too, they're all small. Husband works long hours. And then it occurs to me she might be closer to this than I thought. Because the last time Sheila was home with this partner friend a hers, she saw her next door and reported to me she was Muslim. Because of the headdress thing. She explained there are many headdress types and I said, "It's all Greek to me," and she said, "No, Mom, the Greeks are Orthodox Christian."

After that, there's quite a bit of talk over there. I can hear them on the other side of the wall, raised voices, the way men do, I guess they're just trying to resonate, I mean I don't think he's the next suicide bomber or anything.

I've always been able to hear them through the walls, at night. Foreign sex. Or is it just sex is foreign to me now?

Rumour over the fence from the semi to the south—two nice fellas, insatiable gardeners, their whole backyard is a sand and desert-like motif they call South Beach—they say she's worried about her status. Turns out she's afraid they'll be deported, her and her husband and the kids. Because of the headdress thing.

I see her in the backyard more, restless. She's doing a lot more cooking. The smells that come from that kitchen, wonderful smells, foreign, strong, delicious.

Last week one of her kids was looking at the tomatoes when I looked out.

Sheila shows up from Vancouver middle of October, all defiant about flying the friendly skies for Thanksgiving weekend. Says she's here filming a documentary about a woman stoned to death after being raped, but we both know it's about trying to be close at a time like this. But if I said so I'd get my head bit off.

We have dinner without her partner, who feels threatened, it turns out, by the male presence of Tiffany's live-in, so Tiff doesn't bring him because he's got wind of the rift and chooses to sidestep it like a dog-do altogether. So there's the three of us, all wanting to be with our loved ones instead of each other, and the subject of next door comes up.

"Just when we thought we were safe," Sheila says, "we'll be in burkas."

"Beats sunscreen," Tiffany says. She's always been photosensitive. But this starts Sheila off on one of her lectures that leaves everybody tense, where it turns out all our problems hinge on some decree from the fourteenth-century Christian Church which compelled women to wear hats and gloves because the naked sight of female flesh defiled the sight of God. I don't know what Allah thinks of women, I say.

Then Tiff comes in with an interesting rejoinder. She tells us that our people, unlike their people, can't find religion to save our souls. It turns out we're dropping like flies off the sign of the cross. But them, the more they get shot down, the greater their faith. She saw this picture in the *National Post* of a woman in Palestine—that's next-door neighbours to the Israelites—and she sent her own son on a suicide mission. With her blessing. Happy to see him go. Happy he went to God.

Sheila stands up. "*That* is the ultimate internalized misogyny," she says and I say, "What's that?" and I shouldn't have because I know my ignorance is like a red flag. It was all so black and white in the old days.

"If *anyone* had *bothered* to *ask* the wives of those men who drove the planes," Sheila says, "*one* of them might have opened up, *one* of them might have said, 'My husband is not himself today.' And *that* might have been the beginning of a meaningful dialogue that averted disaster."

Silence.

I guess, basically, Holy Wars elude me.

Mercifully, there's no talk of tomato butter.

No talk of the dishes either, so after the girls leave I go outside and she's out there, standing still as night on their back stoop, her mind wrapped halfway round the world in thought.

So I reach over and pat her hand and I say, don't you worry, you're as Canadian as the rest of us. You can sit on the fence the way we do, and try to see the other guy's point of view till you're cross-eyed with indecision and relieved of the moral responsibility of taking action.

Then I realize I'm starting to sound like Sheila, and I've lost her.

How is it, I say to her, I do all this talking, and still I've got no voice? And it occurs to me it's because nobody's listening. But she seems to be, so I go on.

Why should anybody listen, I ask her, I'm not like Sheila, I haven't got it all worked out.

What do I know about God? I never got religion, I couldn't make it wash. After Bud died Sheila tried to convert me over to "the goddess within." But it seemed whenever I knocked, nobody was home.

Because God only exists for me in little moments, I tell her. Moments of God come, and you just find yourself in them. I mean I don't know exactly, I'm not trying to be Canadian here and skirt the issue, but I think God's different for everybody. And the same, too. It's God when you have great sex—Bud and I had a few, you wouldn't think so—Tiffany wouldn't think so but here's the thing about Sheila, she would. I told Bud my theory one time and after that he'd always ask, "Was it God for you?" And sometimes I'd have to tell him no, I was worshipping at a false idol tonight.

It's God when you share a belly laugh too, the best belly laughs. It was God when I held my girls, both my girls, in my arms, the moment after they were born, and the whole world went breathless. And it was God when Bud died too, just that moment before he went, when he looked at me that one last time as life lifted out of him, and it was just his lips, his lips and his eyes, that said, "goodbye."

Then one of her kids starts crying inside the house, and she reaches over and this time she pats my hand, before she goes in.

And it's after that I realize the house is awful still. Because he's not there. Rumour from South Beach is he's been deported, detained.

It's like *Casablanca*, I tell her one night, round up all the usual suspects. It won't last.

She just shakes her head.

We're two widows.

It's the last weekend in October and they're calling for frost. Sheila calls from Vancouver because it's Halloween—big night for her and her partner in the goddess community. "You should try it, Mom," she says and I say yes, maybe I'll give it a shot.

So I go out to see if the moon is up and she's on their side of the front porch with a letter.

"Is. spell. correct? Is. official?" she says. And she hands me the letter over the big wood divide and I read it and it's a copy of a letter of introduction to the Canadian embassy to say her husband's going back, back to his country to find her brother and bring him home.

Turns out they're not worried about their status. Turns out her brother's legs are missing from a land mine.

I can only find one typo about how he is "messed very much" and it seems stronger to leave it like that so I say, "Yes, it's perfect." And she won't cry, I can tell she won't, she's like our Sheila that way.

Then the moon comes up, and I start to think, it's the tomatoes' last night on earth. And I wonder if, her and me, we couldn't find a recipe.

So I go out to the backyard and I pick them all, a full bushel. And I get her kids to help me drag them through a hole in the fence and she's up there on the stoop, holding the screen door open.

We boil the concoction for hours.

I tell the kids about Halloween and trick-or-treat and outhouses turned over in the country, employing all our sign languages.

On about midnight we each take a spoon and taste the combined recipe for tomato butter. And our eyes meet in heaven.

"Was it God for you?" I say.

"God? Good?" She asks.

"Good god!" The kids all say together.

And her and me and the kids, we laugh and laugh.

END

The Living Library
A *one-act play*
by Linda McCready

Sylvia is a young, enthusiastic woman in search of a career path. As part of a new living library program, she has borrowed a "human book" for an open conversation, but the conversation ends up being one-way.

The Living Library premiered at Alumnae Theatre's New Ideas Festival in Toronto, Ontario, in March of 2014 with the following cast and creative team:

Sylvia	Anne-Marie Krytiuk
Tom	Scott Moulton
Director	Tracy Halloran
Stage Manager	Darcos Chiu

CHARACTER LIST

Sylvia	a bubbly, very talkative twenty-five-year-old woman; dressed casually
Tom	a serious-looking man in his late thirties; wearing a shirt and tie

SETTING

A small boardroom at a local library (table and two chairs).

TIME

The present

A NOTE ON PRODUCTION

Although she is very talkative, Sylvia does not speak very fast. It is more like she is having a conversation with herself.

...

Linda McCready mostly writes comedies/dramatic comedies. Her first full-length play, *The Blunt Widow*, was shortlisted for the Playwrights of Spring provincial playwriting contest in 2008. Her play *Finders Keepers* won second prize at Theatre In the Raw's 2013 Biennial One-Act Playwriting Contest. Her play *Who's Laughing Now* won the adjudicator's Award for Outstanding Original Script at the London One Act Festival in 2015. Linda holds a bachelor's degree in translation and translates her own plays into French. She resides in Burlington and is a member of the Playwrights Guild of Canada.

The Living Library

At rise: TOM *is pacing the room, looking at his watch. After a moment,* SYLVIA *rushes in.*

SYLVIA　　Hi, I'm Sylvia.

TOM　　Hi.

They shake hands.

SYLVIA　　Sorry I'm late.

She puts down her handbag.

I knew I shouldn't have booked your first session 'cause I'm not an early riser. But when I checked the library's website, it was the only time you had free today. Boy, is this new program popular!

They both sit down.

When I read about a collection of "human books" that visitors could borrow for a conversation I thought, "This is awesome!" You see, I'm twenty-five, and I still don't know what I want to be when I grow up. My mom says that I'm a jack of all trades, master of none. She can be so negative! It's true that I have many interests, but

I'm actually very good at many things. I just don't know which one I should focus on. I'm planning to come every Saturday morning to chat with people of all sorts of professions. Today I could have booked the published poet for an inspiring conversation or the female firefighter. She'd have great stories about rescuing people and pets. But I was intrigued by your title—Senior Policy Advisor, and I wondered what it would be like to be a public servant and provide advice to the government. Does it require specific university training or can anyone with good judgment do it?

TOM   Well—

SYLVIA   I think I've got good judgment, but I'm not sure that I'm cut out to work in an office, shuffling papers all day. And as a policy advisor I might have to follow strict policy processes. That could be boring as hell. I'm not a process person. I'm more of a people person. Or maybe I'm wrong, working as a policy advisor might be very exciting. You'll have to tell me all about it.

SYLVIA's cellphone rings.

Sorry. Let me check who is calling.

She looks at the number of the caller.

Got to take this.

She jumps up, steps away, and answers.

Hi, Bryan . . . I can't talk right now. I'm in the middle of an important discussion with someone at the library . . . Yeah, the library . . . I told you yesterday evening. I guess you were too loaded to remember . . . *(in a lower voice, giggling)* I see. Well, you'll just have to take a cold shower . . . See you this evening. Bye, bye.

She hangs up.

My boyfriend. We partied until 2:00 a.m., and he stayed over at my place. He just got up and was looking for me.

She sits down.

Where were we? Oh, yeah, you were about to tell me about your policy advisor job. I read your biography. So you've been with the government for fifteen years. That's a long time! You look like you're about thirty-five. You must have been hired right out of university.

Or maybe you're older. I can see that your hair is thinning. But don't worry about it. You'll look good when you're bald 'cause you have nice features, except for that thing on your cheek. You know, you could have it removed by a dermatologist. I had a similar thing on my neck, and I had it removed. With local anaesthetic I didn't feel a thing.

SYLVIA's cellphone rings.

Sorry.

She jumps up, steps away, and answers.

Hello . . . Oh, hi, Mom . . . I can't chat right now. I'm in the middle of an important conversation with someone at the library . . . I completely forgot about your highlights . . . I could go this afternoon . . . Yeah, four o'clock works for me. Bye, bye.

She hangs up.

My mom.

She sits down.

Wants me to do her hair. I used to work as a hairdresser, but I quit. I enjoyed chatting all day with customers, but I couldn't stand all the smells, the worst were from perms. They really stink, and no one looks good in a perm. Perms should be illegal.

She gestures to TOM to take note of that.

I'm now working as a dog walker. I love dogs! And I don't mind picking up behind six dogs. Not like some people who are squeamish. But it's not a career. I'm also doing volunteer work for a palliative care centre. You may find that surprising, but I like to help people who are dying. At the hospital, I get to sit by the bedside of patients who are very sick. It gives me a chance to chat with them until they take their last breath.

Well, they don't chat much. They're too weak. I do most of the talking. Listening to me talk may tire them out, but at least they're not dying alone ... But I wouldn't want to work in palliative care 'cause I'd have to work at night, and I have a lot of trouble sleeping during the day. I'm very sensitive to light. I pull the drapes, put on a mask, and I still can't sleep. That's my mom's fault. When I was a kid, she always made me sleep in pitch darkness. All that to say that I need to find another career. I've thought of acting. I worked a few times as a film extra. It sounds glamorous, but it's not. I sometimes have to wait hours for a thirty-second shot. But I get to meet many interesting people. Some are very talented, like Joe who can play the harmonica with his feet.

Beat.

You don't seem to find that very impressive, but it's impressive for an eighty-year-old man. Anyway, I gave up acting. I need regular work.

Beat.

Tom, I hate to say it, but you look very stiff. Do you want to loosen up the tie? Let me give you a ten-minute massage.

TOM   No, thanks.

SYLVIA   Don't worry, I'm not making a pass at you.

She gets up, stands behind him, and starts giving him a vigorous back massage.

I took training in massage therapy two years ago, but I didn't complete the program. Couldn't stand the music I was forced to listen to. Made me sleepy. I felt like lying down next to the person on the massage table.

TOM   Please, stop.

SYLVIA's cellphone rings.

SYLVIA   Sorry.

She grabs the phone, steps away, and answers.

Hello . . . I see. *(looks at her watch)* Yeah, I can make it, although I'm having an awesome chat with someone at the library right now . . . Don't worry, I've got what I need in my locker. See you.

She hangs up.

I know this sucks, but I've got to run. I have to be at the YMCA in ten minutes to lead a Latin Funk dance class. I'm an aerobics instructor, but they call me when they're stuck.

I wish we could have had more time to chat. You see. I really don't know what career path to take. I want to make decent money, but I also want to do something that I'm passionate about. I don't mind going back to school, if I have to. I used to get good marks. I'd have no problem being admitted to a university.

One thing I'd like to study is psychology. I already have a good understanding of human nature. Hey, I could become a psychotherapist! I've never thought of that before. Of course, it makes sense 'cause I've got good listening skills. You need good listening skills to work as a psychotherapist. I can imagine myself giving advice to people in distress. I could help them sort their thoughts and develop a positive outlook on life.

I'm not like my mom. I'm a very positive person. I believe that every cloud has a silver lining. As a psychotherapist, I could save lives by preventing people from committing suicide. Now that's meaningful work! The more I think about it, the more I'm convinced that's what I should do. This is so exciting! I've discovered my vocation.

TOM stands.

Thank you so much, Tom, for helping me see the light.

She shakes hands with TOM.

I'll write some good comments on the feedback form at the front desk.

She heads for the door and turns around.

The library needs to know that this program really works! Bye, bye.

SYLVIA heads for the door.

TOM sits down and lets his head drop on the table.

Blackout.

CURTAIN

Flesh Offerings
by Yvette Nolan

A Cree/Métis woman in a Wild West show invites you in to witness: what is real and what is performance?

Flesh Offerings premiered at Sarasvati Productions's International Women's Week Cabaret of Monologues in Winnipeg on March 5, 2013, directed by Hope McIntyre and featuring Melanie Dean.

...

Yvette Nolan is an award-winning playwright, director and dramaturge. Her plays include *BLADE*, *Annie Mae's Movement*, *Job's Wife*, *Scattering Jake*, *from thine eyes*, *Alaska*, *The Birds* (a modern adaptation of Aristophanes's comedy), and *The Unplugging* (winner of the Jessie Richardson Theatre Award for Outstanding Original Script). As a dramaturge, she has worked across Canada on projects including *In Care* by Kenneth T. Williams, *A Soldier's Tale* by Tara Beagan, *Ultrasound* by Adam Pottle, and *A History of Breathing* by Daniel Macdonald. She is currently working with National Arts Centre's French Theatre on a spectacle about Gabriel Dumont's Wild West Show, with Tawata Productions in Wellington, New Zealand, on *Waka/Ciimaan/Vaka*, and with Raven Spirit Dance in Vancouver on *Confluence*. An artistic associate of Signal Theatre, Yvette lives in Saskatoon.

Flesh Offerings

for Marrie

A Cree/Métis woman dressed in a mix of buckskin and nineteenth-century garb. She is adorned with beads and bone. Her hair is in braids. Perhaps she is wearing a blanket as well.

Ladies and gentlemen, boys and girls, welcome to the Wildest West Show! Never mind ol' Buffalo Bill, never mind those cheap knock-offs touring these forty-four excited States of America, this here show, Charles Beveridge's Montana Wildest West Show, is not only the wildest show, it is the realest show you are gonna see. Not to mention none of Beveridge's Indians are complaining to Indian Affairs about ill treatment. Oh no, Charlie takes good care of his Indians.

Oh sure, at first I wasn't keen on the idea—and I sure didn't like that it was that Don Davenport fella who come to talk with us—I'd heard him called The Helena Hustler, and that don't exactly inspire trust in a girl. But ten dollars a month plus board for six months—well, we had to seriously consider that. After all, without land, with fewer and fewer white folks willing to hire Indians, we didn't have a lot of options. Lovely as Montana is, you cannot eat the view.

That ol' Buffalo Bill, he's paradin' Indians all over the country as if we are a vanishing race, but I'm gonna tell you a little secret. We are not vanishing. Uh uh. And here's why.

This here Wildest West Show, we're hiding things insid'a it. All over this country, the politicians and the Indian agents and the missionaries, they're outlawin' ways—no dancing, no sweat lodge, no ceremonies, nothing that has the whiff of spiritual about it. Want us to forget who we are. But here at the Wildest West Show, in amongst the horse races and the re-enactment of the battles and Minos the buckin' bull, between Rattlesnake Jack and Rocky Mountain Kate, there is the sun dance, one of our oldest and most precious practices. You can sit there and watch us as if we're performing what that Reverend fella up in Great Falls calls "a barbaric devilish and defiant act." It'll send chills up and down your spine, ladies, as it does mine.

I'm still not partikalarly comf'rtable *performing* the sun dance for the townsfolk of Pana, Illinois, or Peru, Indiana, or Wapakoneta, Ohio . . . I mean, some things are sacred and should be treated as such . . . and to be dancing and singing and pretending to pierce—well that makes sense because a person can't make a flesh offering every day for months at a time—

But I asked Suzanne, she's been around a long time, she's the one people go to with questions, and if she thinks you really want to know the answer, well then, she'll think on it and tell you what she reckons. So I went over to Suzanne's teepee, and we sat and had a smoke, while Suzanne looked at the stars and the fire and the smoke rising up.

Finally she nods, and she says that even though we're only *performing* the sun dance, that doesn't make it any less important than when we're actually *doing* the sun dance on our own, with the fasting and the preparing, away from the eyes of the *monias*. She says that if we keep the reason for the sun dance in our hearts when we're doing it for the audience, then it's the same as when we're doing it for ourselves. Then she takes a big puff of smoke and lets it out, and says we're never really doing it for ourselves ennaways, are we? We're doing it for our community, for the land, for all our relations.

I am happy to welcome all you fine folks to Beveridge's Montana Wildest West Show here at the Cincinnati Zoo-oh-lah-ji-cal and Botanical Garden. What I have heard some of you fine folks calling a zoo, which is a heck of a lot easier than all those twenty-five-cent words strung together.

I'd never even heard of a zoo until we came to Cincinnati. And I sure as shootin' never seen most of the animals you all keep here—

lions and tigers and that wrinkly giant, the elephant. The skin of that animal looks very tough, but Buffalo Coat rode it, and he said it feels like rough hide, like a tanned buffalo hide. He said when a fly landed on the creature's head, it shook its skin to send the bug away, so it must be as sensitive as you or me.

The men were very excited to see that there are buffalo here at the Cincinnati Zoo. Little Bear spends all his free time down there at the enclosures where they're kept, leaning on the fence, just watching them. Every day when we're getting ready to do the show, I have to send one of the children down to get him. I used to go myself, but the sight of the buffalo makes my heart ache. The keepers take care of them all right, but you can see they're remembering their lives before they were contained.

Now I know the good folks of Cincinnati have been talking about letting us stay here, making our Cree village a permanent part of the Zoo-oh-lah-ji-cal Gardens. That's mighty kind of you. Mighty kind. It'd almost be like having our own land, and that is a powerful temptation. We never signed any treaties, we don't have no reservations, so we're kinda landless, which is why we agreed to go on this Wildest West tour in the first place. Little Bear and Buffalo Coat and the others, they thought the tour was gonna get all the way to Washington, where we'd get to perform for the Great Father. They say he's a good man, a righteous man, and Little Bear thought he might be able to talk with him about getting our own land . . .

But it looks like we're gettin' no further east than this here town, and while we truly appreciate the hospitality of the good folks of Cincinnati, I don't think I want to live in the zoo. I don't mind performing the Wildest West show twice a day, but—

Hidden Bird's death and Papasay's birth—those are things that belong to us.

So step right up, ladies and gentlemen, this way to the bleachers. Ladies, you don't want to sit too close just in case the sharpshooter ain't too sharp tonight. Come in, come on in, tell your friends, because we won't be here forever!

The Only Good Indian
by Jivesh Parasram

A secluded stand-off between a would-be suicide bomber and a police officer. Both present as bearded brown men.

The Only Good Indian was written through support from the Ontario Arts Council Theatre Creators' Reserve program. It was presented as a workshop reading at Actors Repertory Company with support from Cahoots Theatre Company with the following cast:

Bomber	Owais Lightwala
Officer	Jivesh Parasram
Radio	Christopher Stanton

Additional thanks and acknowledgements to Aviva Armour-Ostroff, Marjorie Chan, Indrit Kasapi, Donna-Michelle St. Bernard, Tom Arthur Davis, and Obsidian Theatre Company.

CHARACTER LIST
Bomber
Officer
Radio

...

Jivesh Parasram is a multidisciplinary artist, facilitator, and researcher of Indo-Caribbean descent currently based in Toronto. He is a founding member and the artistic producer of Pandemic Theatre, a core member of the Wrecking Ball, and currently serves as the associate artistic producer for Theatre Passe Muraille. His work both as a playwright and director has played to international audiences. The first graduate of the University of Toronto with a combined focus in Drama and International Relations, Parasram went on to study at both York and Ryerson Universities in the joint graduate program of Communications and Culture. There he spent perhaps much longer than he should have researching the aesthetic philosophy of suicide bombing. He is a member of the Ad Hoc Assembly, a Toronto Arts Council/Banff Centre Cultural Leaders Lab Fellow, and has had the privilege of collaborating with initiatives including Powershift, the Monsoon Festival of Performing Arts, IMPACT, and the SpiderWebShow. Outside of theatre, his writing has been featured in publications including the *Leveller* and CBC.ca.

The Only Good Indian

A secluded back area adjacent to a main street. Something like a back alley or a parking lot. Somewhere "British." In the distance a busy street can be heard. Two bearded brown men wearing vests. BOMBER, *a suicide vest,* OFFICER, *a bulletproof vest. They look very similar.* OFFICER *has been holding* BOMBER *at gunpoint for some time having requested backup. They've been at a standstill for what feels like hours . . .*

BOMBER   No disrespecting, brother, but I don't think you understand how this works.

OFFICER   It's not too late, mate. I can get you out of this.

BOMBER   But I'm already in it, brother. And now so are you. I really think you should just go home.

OFFICER   Just tell me how I can help you. We all get mixed up.

BOMBER   Go home.

OFFICER   I can't do that.

BOMBER   Domestic troubles?

OFFICER   No—I— Do you think this is funny? Do you think anything about this is funny?

BOMBER	Well . . . a little bit. I mean, calling it like I see it, brother, it's a bit silly, isn't it?

Extended silence.

	I don't think your backup's coming.
OFFICER	Look, I know things look bad. Things always look bad.
BOMBER	No, I'm telling you, from here things look hilarious.
OFFICER	This isn't what you have to do.
BOMBER	Yeah, actually it kind of is.
OFFICER	How can you say that?
BOMBER	I don't know if you've noticed, brother, but I kind of got a thing strapped to me here.
OFFICER	Just let me come to you and I can take it off.
BOMBER	That line never worked for me before. Eh? Ya get it? Like with a lady?
OFFICER	Sure. Sure that's funny. You like ladies, huh?
BOMBER	Yeah, they're all right.
OFFICER	Love ladies. I knew it. Lady lovers. I feel ya, mate. Love the . . . the . . . boobs. But you, I bet you're into asses, ya?
BOMBER	What you trying to say?
OFFICER	Well, I mean—
BOMBER	I'm not a batty boy! You're calling me a batty boy, eh?
OFFICER	I am not calling you a batty boy.
BOMBER	I'm all man!
OFFICER	I can see that.
BOMBER	Oh yeah?
OFFICER	You are all man.
BOMBER	That's right, I am.

OFFICER	I bet you've got a massive cock.
BOMBER	What?
OFFICER	I mean—
BOMBER	Are *you* a batty boy?
OFFICER	I'm not— No! No, I'm not.
BOMBER	Hey, brother, it's okay if you are. You know me mate Tony? He's a right bottom. Handsome man too. Not seeing anyone either.
OFFICER	I'm not a batty boy!
BOMBER	It's an ugly thing, brother. I know. The way people talk like it's some sin. Eh, trust me, I'm right proper with God, man, and there is nothing wrong with your life choices.
OFFICER	It is not my life choice!
BOMBER	Right. I'm sorry. It's not a choice. It's who you are, and I think that's beautiful.
OFFICER	I'm not gay! All right?! I'm not gay!
BOMBER	All right!
OFFICER	All right!
BOMBER	Right.
OFFICER	Good.
BOMBER	Little homophobic then?
OFFICER	I'm not— I have gay friends.
BOMBER	Do you?
OFFICER	Yes! Plenty. Tons. Almost all my mates are gays.
BOMBER	Oh yeah?
OFFICER	Yes! I'll have you know. We all hang out. Do gay things. I'm not gay! But I respect the culture.
BOMBER	Is gay a culture?
OFFICER	Sure. Gay bars. Gay ... Pride. The parade. AIDS—
BOMBER	Oh come on!

OFFICER   What? No, not like—it was a unifying thing. The
                 AIDS epidemic was a unifying thing. It brought
                 them together. The gays.

BOMBER   I'm feeling a little uncomfortable, brother.

OFFICER   Then why don't you let me come over there and
                 take that off you.

          OFFICER *approaches,* BOMBER *flinches,* OFFICER *steps back.*

                 OK! OK! I'm staying where I am.

BOMBER   You should leave, brother! You should leave now!

OFFICER   *(into radio)* Officer Singh reporting. Where are we
                 with that backup? Do you copy?

          Silence.

BOMBER   They're not gonna come, brother.

OFFICER   They're— You! You stop speaking right now!

          Silence.

                 (into radio) This is Officer Singh reporting.
                 Requesting backup. Respond!

          Silence.

                 Fuck! OK! Look, I need you to work with me.

          Silence.

                 What's your name, then?

BOMBER   I can talk then? You're not gonna shoot me then?

OFFICER   Yes. Look, I'm Sandeep. What's your name?

BOMBER   Marvin.

OFFICER   Seriously?

BOMBER   What you think just cause I got a bomb strapped
                 to me I got a Muslim name?

OFFICER   I didn't say that.

BOMBER   Mohammed? Ya? Or like Aziz? Right? Or fucking
                 Ibn-Jihad? Ya?

OFFICER	Look, I just— I didn't think your name would be Marvin.
BOMBER	Ya, well it ain't easy then, is it? With a silly name like that. Oh, hi, Mash'Allah brothers, I'm Marvin. No, I'm a proper right jihadi, ya? Hate the haram motherfuckers! Oh—ye—right well me dad just really had a thing for Marvin Gaye.
OFFICER	*(laughs)*
BOMBER	Eh? See, man! Told you, this whole mess is proper fucked, ya? *(laughs)* Pretty silly thing, this.
OFFICER	Your name's actually Marvin?
BOMBER	As I live and breathe . . . Well, for now, right?
OFFICER	Unreal.
BOMBER	Stranger than friction, brother.

Brief pause.

OFFICER	Look you seem like a rational man, Marvin.

MARVIN *looks down at the bomb.*

BOMBER	You all right in the head?
OFFICER	Why are you doing this?

Pause.

BOMBER	Proper Jihad, brother Sandeep. Mujahideen and shit.

Silence.

OFFICER	Right. Mujahideen.
BOMBER	God's soldier.
OFFICER	Right. Virgins, all that.
BOMBER	Sexy ones.
OFFICER	Right.
BOMBER	And they're like experienced virgins, brother.
OFFICER	. . . That makes absolutely no sense.
BOMBER	I know! Like you ask yourself, how could they

be experienced if they're virgins? But they are! Been trained by magic and shit.

OFFICER   Oh yeah?

BOMBER   Oh yeah.

Silence.

OFFICER   You know I've always respected Islam.

BOMBER   Me too. It's the shit.

OFFICER   Ya. Ya, it's the shit.

BOMBER   Love it.

OFFICER   Right . . . Say, what's Mohammed's uncle's name again?

Silence.

You know, the major trader? Took him in after his mother died? Really impacted his life. Tried to protect him? I just . . . what was his name again?

Silence.

Right.

BOMBER   You're a funny man, eh?

OFFICER   Well we're both pretty fucked here, aren't we? Actually I can see the humour now. Stranger than *fiction*! You know . . . I think his name was Marvin. That sounds right.

BOMBER   You think they can tell the difference? That they give a flying fuck? Why do you think they abandoned you, brother?

OFFICER   They did not abandon me.

BOMBER   No, they've got the place surrounded. Hear those sirens?

Silence.

The only good Indian's a dead Indian, ya?

OFFICER   I don't know what happened to you. To make you

feel the way you do. I really— But we can talk if
you want to talk.

Silence.

These days. We gotta be patient. I know.
Sometimes they just . . . the climate . . . the bigots
. . . I get so . . . But you gotta trust that things
will get better. We gotta be better because most
people aren't . . . they don't think like . . . It's not
that bad. All right? Big picture. It's really not that
bad.

BOMBER   Oh yes, now, Officer Sahib![1]

OFFICER   Don't—

BOMBER   Officer Sahib and bullshit Shaheed!

OFFICER   I'm proud of who I am. You should be too.
Brothers, right? OK.

BOMBER   Oh, I'm proud brother. I'm glad you are too. You
know? Really. But they don't know who you are.
They don't know who I am. Take one look and
we're all just the— How many brothers are they
gonna make mistake after mistake with, brother?
You read the news—hell, you make the news.

OFFICER   I'm not going to pretend like it's perfect. It's not.
Look I'm not supposed to . . . There's—we need
to work on more disciplinary—

BOMBER   Slap that wrist! I mean, it's civil. Right? Way
you all deal internally? Leave of absence for the
murderers when it's for Queen and Country! And
why not? It's freedom, right? You can say whatever
the fuck you want, just don't you dare wear hijab
while you do it!

OFFICER   That's why? That's not even—

BOMBER   No. It's 'cause my daddy touched me. No, no. It's
'cause of the virgins. Really it's the virgins. No,
really? Really it's 'cause they keep dogs as pets.
No! No! It's 'cause they let women vote.

---

1   Here, "Sahib" means holder, master . . . or otherwise native informant.

	No, really. Really it's cause of Israel, brother. It's cause they—
OFFICER	All right I get it.
BOMBER	I don't think you do! 'Cause if you got it, brother, you wouldn't be pointing a gun at me.
OFFICER	What difference would it make?
BOMBER	'Cause I choose. Not you. Not them. I choose when. I choose how. It's gotta be me. You wanna take that away from me? Then you're just like them, brother. And I don't want to kill one of us too. One's already too many, and you can just go home.
OFFICER	You wanna choose. Fine. Choose. But if you do this you won't just kill yourself. You walk into that road? All those people are innocent—
BOMBER	They're not! And neither are you. And neither am I. We live here. We live here and we don't stop them from blowing up cousin Salman's wedding, do we? No, we just sell them a mango lassi and a fucking jalfrezi.
OFFICER	They didn't ask—
BOMBER	Nobody asked! It's just equalizing. You know bombs 'n shit, they go off all the time back home, ya? All over fucking Desi-stan. That's just what they do, isn't it? Italians have siesta. Brown people blow up—
OFFICER	. . . Actually, siesta's a Spanish—
BOMBER	Shut up!! So this is just cultural exchange. Happy multicultural day, brother. Time for the costume parade.

Pause. BOMBER glances to the street. He does not move.

| | S'only right to give 'em a taste of what they sow. |
| OFFICER | This isn't gonna change— |

BOMBER   It's not supposed to change anything! It's just fair, man.

          Silence. They wait.

OFFICER   Guyana.

BOMBER   What?

OFFICER   Me. Guyanese. When you say back home . . . Not me, mate. Guyanese.

BOMBER   *(laughs)*

OFFICER   Not Desi enough for you?

BOMBER   Oh! Hit a nerve?

OFFICER   We didn't choose to end up there. You think I don't feel what you're saying? Marvin! You darker than me, Marvin?!

BOMBER   *(laughs)* Right. Guyanese.

OFFICER   Guyanese.

          Pause.

BOMBER   Trini.

OFFICER   What?

BOMBER   *(laughs)* Me. Trini. Know what else?

OFFICER   What?

BOMBER   Christian.

OFFICER   *(laughs)*

BOMBER   Pentecostal. *(laughs)*

OFFICER   Boy, ya real full of shit, nah? *(laughs)*

BOMBER   *(schups, then laughs)*

OFFICER   All yuh cya even make a good roti.[2]

BOMBER   What yuh crack? All yuh doh know—[3]

OFFICER   Hold ya—[4]

---

2   You all can't even make a good roti.
3   Are you crazy? You don't know—
4   Shut your—

Sniper rifle gunshot. OFFICER *has been shot from behind. He falls dead.*

RADIO

Shot confirmed. Repeat: target is down. Officer Singh, report. Officer Singh. Report. Officer— Aw shit. Singh? Aw shit! Fuck. Fuck me! Fuck . . . OK . . . Fuuuuck . . .

BOMBER

Real good, brother. Real good.

END

A *Friend for Life*
by Talia Pura

When Kristy's boyfriend comes out as gay and breaks up with her, she takes it very personally. How could her parents have always known he was gay, when she didn't? Her mother tries to help her process her feelings and Kristy comes to the realization that this isn't a reflection on her at all, but an opportunity to be a friend.

A *Friend for Life* is part of a full-length play called *Perfect Love*, which has received a public reading in Sarasvàti Productions's FemFest 2013, and a workshopped reading with the Manitoba Association of Playwrights in 2015.

CHARACTER LIST

Kristy	seventeen years old
Cheryl	early fifties, her mother
Frank	early fifties, her father

SETTING

A living room

...

Talia Pura is an author, performer, and filmmaker. She's written over twenty-five plays and performed many of her solo dramas, including *Confessions of an Art School Model*, in major North American cities. Several of her screenplays and plays, including *Cry After Midnight*, were written based on her experiences in Afghanistan with the Canadian Forces Artists Program. Talia's work has also been published in *Prairie Fire* and *a/cross sections: New Manitoba Writing*, and she has written, produced, and directed nine short dramatic films, which have played at various festivals around the world. She is the author of *STAGES: Creative Ideas for Teaching Drama* and *CUES: Theatre Training & Projects from Classroom to Stage*, published by J. Gordon Shillingford Publishing, and the picture book *Alexia Wants to Fly*. She lives in Sante Fe, New Mexico.

A *Friend for Life*

KRISTY is curled up on the sofa, Kleenex in hand, sobbing her eyes out. CHERYL enters.

CHERYL Hey, hey, hey, what's the matter? *(She sits beside her and puts an arm around her shoulders.)*

KRISTY *(crying harder)* Oh, Mom.

CHERYL What is it, Kristy? What happened? *(figures it out)* Where's Matthew?

KRISTY Ohhhhh, he, he, he left. *(more tears)*

CHERYL You two broke up?

KRISTY Not, not exactly, but I guess so.

CHERYL What does that mean?

KRISTY He told me he was gay!

CHERYL Oh.

KRISTY So, I guess we broke up.

CHERYL I guess so.

KRISTY Last week, he told me he loved me, and today he tells me he's gay.

CHERYL	Well, he can be gay and still care about you.
KRISTY	No, he doesn't care about me at all. How can he?
CHERYL	Well, I'm sure that his feelings for you—
KRISTY	Oh my god! I'm his last girlfriend.
CHERYL	Yes, I suppose you are.
KRISTY	Great, just great!
CHERYL	You sound angry about that.
KRISTY	Well, yeah! What are people going to say about me?
CHERYL	Why should people say anything about—
KRISTY	They'll say that I am the worst girlfriend ever.
CHERYL	Oh, honey, that's not—
KRISTY	I've turned him!
CHERYL	Noooo—
KRISTY	How am I ever going to live this down? Why couldn't he just say that he changed his mind, that he just didn't want to be tied down, that he found someone else? Why did he have to tell me he's gay?
CHERYL	I think it means that he cares about you, and trusts you with this, this secret, that he's probably carried with him for some time.
KRISTY	No, I doubt that. He's just being a jerk.
CHERYL	Why would you say that?
KRISTY	Mother, we had sex. He wasn't gay when we had sex.
CHERYL	Well, he could have been. He just hadn't quite figured out his feelings yet, at that time.
KRISTY	I'm so embarrassed! How will I ever live this down?
CHERYL	Kristy. This really isn't about you.

KRISTY	Of course it is. This is going to get around and I'll be the laughingstock of the whole school!
CHERYL	Now listen. He is the same nice guy that you brought home six months ago. The fact that he's come out about being gay has nothing to do with you, or what kind of girlfriend you might have been. He cared about you enough to tell you the truth. Now, you have to be mature about this, and support him.
KRISTY	Support him? With everyone laughing at me?
CHERYL	No one is going to be laughing at you.
KRISTY	They'll think it's my fault that he's gay.
CHERYL	No one is going to think that. The only way that anyone will say anything bad about you is if you start talking about him and saying the things that you just said to me.
KRISTY	But—
CHERYL	Now, I know that you were surprised by this, and you were reacting out of hurt. That's okay, you are entitled to your feelings.
KRISTY	Right. He made me feel bad and—
CHERYL	And you got those feelings out appropriately, to me, who will not repeat them to anyone else.
KRISTY	But they are my feelings!
CHERYL	Fine, they're out. Now take the high road. Support him, be his friend. That's what he needs now.
KRISTY	His friend? After what he did—
CHERYL	Kristy! Stop! For the last time, he didn't do this to you. He didn't set out to hurt you.

FRANK enters.

FRANK	What's going on?
CHERYL	Matthew just broke up with Kristy.
FRANK	Oh, did he come out of the closet?

KRISTY   Dad!

FRANK   What?

KRISTY   He told you he was gay?

FRANK   He didn't have to. Cheryl, what did I tell you when she brought that kid home?

CHERYL   Frank, maybe this isn't the—

FRANK   I said, well, she's going to have a friend for life. Didn't I say that? Huh?

CHERYL   Yes, Frank, that's what you said.

KRISTY   So, what, you always thought that Matthew was gay?

CHERYL   We thought he might be, dear.

KRISTY   Why didn't you tell me?

FRANK   What good would that have done?

KRISTY   You could have warned me.

CHERYL   If you were older, if he was proposing to you, then maybe, but—

KRISTY   So you thought you'd just wait and let him dump me?

CHERYL   We didn't know how long it might take him to figure things out for himself. You're only seventeen. You might have broken up for any number of reasons before that.

KRISTY   So there it is. My parents could tell that my boyfriend was gay and I couldn't.

CHERYL   We weren't sure, dear.

FRANK   Oh yes we—

CHERYL   Matthew told you that he still wanted to be friends, right?

KRISTY   Yes.

CHERYL   Well, wasn't he always very kind and sweet to you?

KRISTY	Yes.
CHERYL	So, won't he make a great friend?
KRISTY	Yeah, I guess so.
CHERYL	Well then, you've got a great friend, maybe for life.
KRISTY	We didn't actually have sex.
CHERYL	Hmm.
KRISTY	But we almost did.
CHERYL	Uh-huh.
KRISTY	But then he remembered he had homework due, and so we stopped and he went home. Argggg. I'm such an idiot.

FRANK snorts. CHERYL gives her a hug.

CHERYL	No, no you are not. You are a bright, warm, intelligent young woman and a fabulous daughter. And now you'll be a wonderful friend to someone who really could use your support. Things aren't going to be easy for him, you know?
KRISTY	Yeah, you're right. I don't think he's told anyone else yet.
CHERYL	Well, you can feel honoured that you were the first.
KRISTY	I guess.
FRANK	You're going to be okay, kiddo. I hope that the next straight guy you bring home is as nice as Matthew . . . and is equally disinterested in having sex with you.
KRISTY	Dad!
FRANK	You've got time, sweetheart. Lots of time.

THE END

An Ordinary Guy
by Ann Snead

Jeff's an ordinary guy, not interested in causes or protests, but he knows as well as anyone the environment is in trouble. What bothers him most is when field-grown summer tomatoes, his favourite food, disappear. Except for one, in his neighbour's garden. Will he let it be, with its superior, disease-resistant genes, or will temptation prove too much for him?

An Ordinary Guy was broadcast by CFBU-St. Catharines and presented by Playwrights Niagara in association with @ the Museum Thursday Night in 2015 with the following cast and creative team:

Jeff   John Jacobs

Director   Ann Snead
Staging   Tina Yeung-Moore

CHARACTER LIST
Jeff   A forty-something man

SETTING
Bathroom with toilet and hamper. A window in the background.

TIME
Near future; about eight-thirty in the morning. Helen has just left for school with the girls. Jeff himself will be going off to work shortly.

...

Ann Snead is a Niagara-based playwright with an interest in exploring social issues as they affect the individual. Her aim in her writing is to be both witty and thought-provoking. Her works include *The Jigsaw Puzzle* (Theatre Aquarius, Hamilton), *Choices* (Regina Little Theatre), *The Room* (Theatre Beyond Words, St. Catharines), and *A Touch of Beauty* (InspiraTO Festival, Toronto). Her two most recent plays are *Augustine Pursued* and *RippleEffect*, which was workshopped by Road Less Traveled Productions in Buffalo, NY. More information and samples of her work can be found at www.annsnead.com.

An Ordinary Guy

JEFF is standing by the bathroom window. He peeks through the blinds, then turns to the audience.

JEFF

I'm your ordinary guy. Wife, two kids. House, two cars. I know there are problems in the world, but I try not to let them get me down. Live and let live, that's my motto. I'm not interested in politics. Never been on a protest march. Never signed a petition. I just keep my head down; get on with life.

He sits—fully clothed—on the toilet, pulling the laundry hamper into place in front of him.

'Course I know something's going on with the environment. I don't need Greenpeace to tell me. I mean, me and the girls go camping and it's hard not to notice things are different. A fine spring day. The boardwalk. Skunk cabbage erupting out of the mud. Shiny yellow marsh-marigolds. Trees dripping with catkins. Perfect, except . . . it's quiet. At first I don't know what I'm listening for. Then I realize it's frogs. Bullfrogs. Spring peepers. I remember when frogs equalled spring. The noise was almost deafening, until you got too close. Then things'd go quiet for a while. Never had much luck seeing the adults, but every pond, every puddle, was full of tadpoles. Was. But not now.

Then there were the birds. Some didn't come back from wherever it was they migrated to. Some died of viruses nobody'd ever heard of—you'd find their bodies under a tree, maybe, or floating along the shore. Some just seemed to disappear. Didn't affect me directly, though. Just meant no dawn chorus. Meant I could sleep in longer in the morning.

A car door slams. He jumps up and checks the window, then sits back down.

Anyhow, as I was saying, it was clear things were changing, but not enough to affect me. Then bees started dying. Suddenly the Net was full of articles about "colony collapse disorder." I didn't pay much attention. There are a lot of farms in this area, but I'm not a farmer. Don't know anyone who is. Turns out, though, that farmers need bees to pollinate their crops, and what everyone thought was just a temporary problem, wasn't. Corn was OK. Wheat. Everything else grew and flowered, but didn't set fruit the way it used to. Food started to get expensive. Ordinary food. Things like apples and almonds, blueberries and broccoli.

He takes a container from the hamper and puts it on the floor.

Have to admit I've never liked fruit and veggies. Oh, I eat them, all right, my wife sees to that. But I don't really like them. Except for tomatoes. I didn't care one way or the other about tomatoes when we lived further south, and you could grow them practically all year round. But somehow, once I had a decent *insalata di caprese*—in a sports bar in Toronto, after a Jays game—I couldn't get enough of them. Don't have room to grow them—we have a pool—but that never used to matter. Friends would give them to us, and for a few weeks in late summer . . . heaven. For the rest of the year, it was canned. The ones that're picked green and shipped in . . . or the hydroponic ones . . . they weren't worth eating. Only vine-ripened ones have that special flavour. It's been a long time since I had one of those.

He takes a cutting board and knife out of the hamper and arranges them carefully.

Before, if I found a bushel of tomatoes at the farmers' market for a good price, I'd gorge on them. Now I can't find them at all. Turns out, you see, that there's some kind of blight that affects them and potatoes and makes them go all black and mushy. The same blight that caused the Irish Famine. My neighbour explained it to me. The disease isn't caused by a virus or bacteria or mould, but by something called a protist. Pro-tist. What the hell's that? Anyway, it started in the Northeast. Spread from field to field, farm to farm, country to country, continent to continent. It's mutated. Become resistant to all the sprays we've got.

Very carefully, he opens the container and looks in.

Ever had a real craving for something? Like beer on a hot summer's day? Ever looked at something and wanted it so bad you could almost taste it?

Out rolls a tomato.

I've been watching this little lady grow. We have a relationship, she and I. And now she's ready to give herself to me. A few days earlier, and I'd've had to fry her. Ever had fried green tomatoes? Very nice, but second-best.

He caresses the tomato lovingly. He smells it, closing his eyes and inhaling deeply.

What does a tomato smell like? It smells like . . . a tomato. It smells like . . . summer days in the backyard, barbecuing burgers. It smells like pizza after the game.

What's your favourite way of eating tomatoes? In a salad? As soup or juice? In spaghetti or pizza? If you thought this was going to be the last tomato you ever ate, how would you eat it? With salt? Or without?

He takes out a salt shaker.

Wonder what they're doing in Italy, without tomatoes. Maybe they've got synthetic ones, like we do. They're made out of . . . well, I don't know what they're made out of. They look perfect. They taste like . . . crap. But this *(pointing to what's on the cutting board)* is the real thing. Where did I get it from, you ask? *(putting his finger to his lips)* Don't ask.

He poses the tomato artistically, using his cellphone to take pictures of it.

Isn't it beautiful? Look at it. Look at it closely. The colour. Red melting into orange. Light green—no, lime green on the shoulders. The stem—dark green, holding on with—count them—one, two, three, four, five clasps. Clasps that look like the claws of a hawk.

He takes a paper napkin and tucks it in at his neck. He starts to cut the tomato, hesitates, then starts again.

Finally he cuts it into pieces. He salts one.

What does the inside of a tomato look like? Those little seeds—what colour are they? Yellow. Green.

He closes his eyes and takes a bite. He looks close to having an orgasm.

Hints of hot August days.

A police siren. His eyes fly open. He peeks through the blind; the noise recedes; he settles back.

I said people couldn't grow tomatoes anymore because of the blight. That's not completely true. If you've got a greenhouse, you can try sealing it off. Can't use bumblebees anymore—they're gone—but there's something called the Electric Bee—a kind of wand—that you can use to move pollen from one flower to the other. Obviously you can't do it by the acre—unless you pay Chinese wages—but, high demand, low supply—you can get a good price for whatever you can produce. Better than nothing, I suppose—and a lot better than the synthetic stuff—but if you closed your eyes, you might not guess you were eating a tomato.

He eats another piece, savouring it.

There's a lot of research going on to find a blight-resistant tomato for commercial use. My neighbour works at the Vineland Research Station. The guys there think they've finally come up with one. VRS 2890. The number tells you how many varieties they've discarded. All of them patented. There's a lot of money—

His cellphone rings. He looks at who it is.

Speak of the devil . . .

He turns it off.

I can see his backyard from my window. *(pointing)* This window. He's got a big vegetable garden. Rows and rows of tomatoes. This year, all his plants rotted. Except for one. One plant with one tomato on it. He was going to save the seeds and use them in field trials next year. If he could develop a new, *resistant* strain, he'd be famous. And rich.

He checks the message.

He's hysterical.

He listens.

Seems all the plants at the research station died. That plant, that tomato, was the only one that survived. He's asking if I know anything about where it got to.

He looks thoughtfully at the last piece of tomato.

I could have tomatoes for the rest of my life. *(beat)* But I'd be eating them in jail. *(beat)* Maybe I could make a deal . . .

He stares intently at the tomato.

But why take a chance?

He gobbles up the last slice, sighs, licks his fingers. He wipes the board and blade with toilet paper and tosses that and his napkin underneath him. He stands up.

Blackout and sound of a flush.

Say the Words
by Donna-Michelle St. Bernard

Everything you've heard about feminists is totally true.

Say the Words was written for Wrecking Ball 16: #YesAllWomen, staged at The Theatre Centre in Toronto, directed by Rebecca Burton and featuring Viv Moore, Amanda Cordner, and Virgilia Griffith.

CHARACTER LIST

Ava   a senior official
Bea   a career agent
Doli   a new recruit

A NOTE ON THE TEXT

If desired, pop culture references may be updated.

A NOTE ON STYLE

Inspired by *Labyrinth*, *Dr. Strangelove*, and *The West Wing*.

...

Donna-Michelle St. Bernard, aka Belladonna the Blest, is an emcee, playwright, and arts administrator.

Her works for the stage include *Dark Love*, *They Say He Fell*, *A Man A Fish*, *Cake*, *The House You Build*, *Salome's Clothes*, and *Gas Girls*. DM's work has been recognized through a SATAwards nomination, the Herman Voaden Playwriting Competition, an Enbridge playRites Award, a Dora Mavor Moore Award for Outstanding New Play, the Victor Martyn Lynch-Staunton Award, and two nominations for the Governor General's Literary Award.

She has developed work through residencies at Obsidian Theatre, Dynamo Theatre, the National Arts Centre, Theatre Passe Muraille, lemonTree creations, the Stratford Festival Playwrights Retreat, the Banff Playwrights Colony, and the Banff Spoken Word program.

DM is a true believer.

Say the Words

Somewhere in a secret bunker, BEA *and* DOLI *are tapped into a listening apparatus.* AVA *is supervising the operation.* BEA *gets* AVA's *attention.*

BEA	I think we have a Code Areola, Agent Ava. Sensitive target. This one knows too much.
DOLI	How is that possible?
BEA	I don't know, but he seems to have a lot of inside knowledge.
DOLI	Can we take him out? Let me take him out.
AVA	No, you know the rules. Not unless he says the words.
DOLI	But it's so close.
AVA	Tell me. What did he say . . . exactly?
BEA	I've got it here. He said, "These women are feminazis, making all men disenfranchised citizens."
AVA	Uh-huh. "These women." Close, but no. Leave him. Just keep listening. We have to have

patience; bide our time unless they force our hand. Unless they say the words exactly.

DOLI   Look! Our latest hashtag is trending like crazy. Have you ever seen anything like it?

BEA   Not since we took back the night.

AVA   How are we coming with the next phase of that, anyways?

BEA   We agreed to go incremental, so we're taking back the morning next and then the noontime. Soon we will have all of time itself.

AVA   Wonderful. Morning, noon, and night. Three makes a full set.

ALL   Accessorize!

BEA   All of time itself. All for us.

DOLI   How are we alerting the Junior Squadrons to the new strategies?

BEA   Instructions have been coded into the lyrics of a new single by Justin Bieber—I mean, undercover agent Lulubelle. That brave little lesbian is making the greatest sacrifice.

ALL   For the team!

BEA   For the Worldwide Feminazi Federation, an international cabal which includes every woman and girl in the world, living or dead. (All hail Princess Di.)

AVA   Here's to our national leader, Kathleen Wynne.

DOLI   And here's to pathologically hating all men in the world for no reason, even though they never did anything to us ever.

BEA   Just a bunch of darn nice guys.

DOLI   Hear, hear!

AVA   You'll go far in this organization. Now, where's Agent Danis?

DOLI   She's revising textbooks to conceal how history has always been in our favour.

BEA   Oh, and we've updated the list of words.

DOLI   You mean the made-up words we arbitrarily start using all of a sudden, and act like they've always been around, so anyone who doesn't use them looks like a caveman? Tell her what's new.

BEA   I'm adding *pro-rape*, changing *miscegenation* to *ms.–cegenation*, and I thought we'd try out *labia-ratory*—that's a place where lady scientists work.

AVA   Great. Everything is on course. Soon we'll have a full on vagigarchy.

DOLI   What next?

BEA   Pillow fight!

DOLI and BEA pull out their ever-ready pillows.

AVA   No! We all want to, but there's no time to waste! We've successfully got women reporting pro sports from inside the men's locker room, thereby doubling our territory in that region faster than the founding of the WNBA. We have to take advantage of the ground we've gained to establish momentum. Doli, Bea, skew the statistic to "prove" that we make less money than men for doing the same work.

DOLI   Skewing the stats.

BEA   Skew 'em!

AVA   Hack into the annals of academia to fabricate an imbalance between women's scholarly performance and available employment opportunities in their chosen fields.

DOLI   Hacking academia.

BEA   Hack the ack!

AVA   Now brainwash little boys to be unnaturally attached to their mothers well into adulthood,

215

ignoring the insidious damage we inflict with our soft, pansy-ass child-rearing.

DOLI   Brainwashing the kids.

BEA   Scrub-a-dub-dub!

AVA   And our lady researchers have infiltrated the superior facilities of Garnier Fructis. They're applying all that advanced technology to make sperm unnecessary to reproduction.

BEA   This is so great. Once we don't need their seed, we'll all be able to lez out together forever!

DOLI   Yay!

BEA   Pillow fight!

BEA and DOLI pull out pillows, then notice AVA's pensive expression.

DOLI   What are you looking at, Ava?

AVA   Mammary Report. Two solid victories for the breast-ocracy: topless women in the streets and legal public breastfeeding have both officially normalized.

BEA   Ingenious.

AVA   If we can dangle enough bait in front of them, we'll entrap them into wolf whistles, ass slaps, and bingo-bango: class-action lawsuits.

BEA   Don't we have enough money yet?

DOLI   I thought that's why we created alimony.

BEA   Oh, no. We stopped relying on that strategy when Oprah became treasurer. But surely she has most of it by now.

AVA   No! We need to get *all* the money. Only then can we activate the Vulvitron, emasculating all of mankind with one flip of the switch.

DOLI   Well, the Girl Scouts are picking up the slack since we lost Martha, but according to these figures we still can't afford to stop filing frivolous suits.

BEA   Is there any chance that we'll hurt legitimate sexual harassment lawsuits?

AVA   Ha! No such thing. I contrived the concept of harassment in 1974 to annoy executives.

BEA   That was you?

AVA   Some of my best work. Frankly I can't believe it hasn't fizzled out.

DOLI   Poor Clarence Thomas.

BEA   Darn nice guy.

AVA   I also invented slut-shaming, gender binary, and informed consent.

BEA   Damn, you're good.

AVA   And I'm working on designing a jockstrap with painful but "necessary" underwire support. Know what that's gonna feel like?

BEA   Nuts in a vise!

DOLI   Wow. You guys are always working so hard. Do you ever have any time for dreaming?

AVA   Oh, I've got dreams.

BEA   Me, too. I dream about having abortions. As many as possible. You know, because they're so pleasant. Sometimes, I'm not even pregnant and I just want to have an abortion anyway. *(sigh)* One day it will all be possible.

AVA   My dream is a jar of shrivelled sacs on every mantle. All squished up in there, like little oysters without their shells, trapped and vulnerable.

DOLI   Sometimes I dream about maybe making it through my whole life without being raped.

AVA & BEA   Mmm. Yeah.

BEA	What's the matter, Doli? You look glum.
DOLI	I just wish girls didn't have to go through the charade of school at all. I envy those Afghan girls.
AVA	I know, I know. But getting an education, getting the vote, fighting for status in the churches and other institutions, forcing them to give us things we don't even want, it's not just for spite. All these painful sacrifices have a function, aside from creating a helpful diversion.
BEA	I wish I knew that we would see the rewards within my lifetime.
AVA	Come on, womyn-with-a-"y." You know the Committee has decided to wait until hard-working men have dug up every last mineral from the earth. Otherwise we'd have to do it all ourselves, with our hands, down in the dirty dirt with the worms and icky bugs.
BEA & DOLI	Ewww.
AVA	But there's good news. Looks like we're about two weeks away from extracting the very last non-renewable resource. Then we'll have no further use for them. We can all get on our yoga pants and put Operation Juicy Cleanse into action.
DOLI	There's something I don't understand: how on earth did they fail to see this coming?
BEA	No one knows. We were so obvious about the whole scheme, yet we seem to be getting away with it right under their noses.
AVA	For that we can thank the Internet. I've done some research. They had their prophets, vocal ones, but the dark truth was drowned out by a profusion of YouTube cats—good job, Agent Doris!
BEA	We've been watching maddox@xmission for three years now. If only men had better listening skills, they'd hear his dangerous truth.

AVA	Ah, yes. When he said that we should "Put on our bras, shave our armpits, and quit bitching," I thought he had us for sure.
BEA	And when he revealed the dark truth that "women get paid less than men because they prefer different lifestyles . . ." It was so right on the money, I almost shit my pants.
DOLI	That's why we have to take him out! Let me at him, boss.
AVA	Doli, try to control your histrionic blood lust.

BEA gets an alert from her terminal.

BEA	Shh shhh. I think I've got one.
DOLI	eatadick@yahoo.com? I knew it. What's he say?
BEA	Hold on. I'm scrolling . . . "Gay . . . you're gay . . . check out this bunch of gays . . . fuck these dykes . . . you're just jealous no one wants to rape you . . . standard stuff . . . blah . . . blah . . . blah" . . . and pay dirt. "All women are feminazis."
DOLI	To which suckacock@hotmail.com replies, "All women?"
BEA	And eatadick says, "Yes, all women."
DOLI	He said it, dammit! He said the words!
BEA	The jig is up.
DOLI	Can I go get him? Can I?
AVA	Get him. Get them all.
BEA	All of them?
AVA	Yes. All men. Hit the switch. It's Vulvitron time.

The Vulvitron is activated, changing the whole world.

	I told you, they had their chance. Now we have all the power.
DOLI	What are we gonna do with it?

AVA   . . . I think I'm gonna go walk to the store. Right through the park.

> AVA *leaves,* BEA *and* DOLI *look after her in admiration, then follow.*

END

Steps
by José Teodoro

People silently fret in formal wear. A bell rings. Everyone rises and begins to dance with invisible partners to Miles Davis's "Flamenco Sketches," inspiring reveries on solitude, loneliness, cities, and secret connections. The music, the dancing, the reveries: everything seeks suspension. Longing is like smoke.

Steps premiered at Vancouver's Upintheair Theatre's inaugural Walking Fish Festival, directed and produced by Heidi Taylor and featuring Patricia J. Collins, Stephanie Hayes, Aiden Maxted, Jennifer A. Rozylo, and Paul Ternes.

A NOTE ON PRODUCTION
What you're gonna need
1. At least five actors
2. Some chairs
3. Formal wear
4. A window, maybe, with rain
5. A copy of Miles Davis's "Flamenco Sketches," the last track on *Kind of Blue*—and use the version that made it on the record, not the alternate take.

...

José Teodoro is the author of the plays *Mote, Cloudless, The Tourist, The Vultures, Husk,* and *Slowly, an exchange is taking place.* He writes essays, reviews, and interviews about film and literature for such publications as *Cinema Scope, The Globe and Mail, Film Comment, National Post, Brick,* and *subTerrain.* José is the co-author, with Mexican photographer Laura Barrón, of *Cathedral,* a three-metre-long book of text and photography. José has served on juries for the Montreal, Havana, Seattle, Toronto, Guadalajara, Mannheim-Heidelberg, Thessaloniki, Reykjavík, and Fribourg film festivals. He has worked in film as a scenarist, story editor, actor, and producer. He also writes and edits program notes for the Toronto, Panama, and Miami International Film Festivals. José has been artist-in-residence at several institutions, including the Banff Centre for Arts and Creativity, the Canadian Film Centre, Toronto's Gibraltar Point, Seattle's Annex Theatre, and Vancouver's Playwrights Theatre Centre. He is currently at work on *Nothing But Time,* a book of essays and conversations with renowned Swiss-Canadian filmmaker Peter Mettler, and *Island,* a new play set in 1983, 1999, and 2015.

Steps

The following speeches are to be stretched across the allotted times with the actors just feeling their way through as they dance with imaginary partners. A lingering space here, a flurry of words there: just let the music and the movement carry you wherever it feels natural. Try to keep dancing. If you can play with a more "modal" approach to the material, so much the better. The allotted time spans are only guidelines. Don't worry about it too much.

–0.00

The late afternoon rain is chilly, but we keep pretty warm. If you look inside that window over there, you'll see some people sitting, waiting.

The men hunch over in their wrinkled tuxedoes. Their chairs look uncomfortable, or maybe it's just the way they're sitting in them. None of the men make eye contact with anybody. At least one of them is smoking. There's this one guy that can't stop sweating. All of them look a little anxious.

The women wear a variety of slightly awkward, overly adorned evening gowns. None look particularly happy about it. Some sit straight, some slouch. When one catches a glimpse of another, they smile awkwardly and look away quickly.

A bell rings. Everyone gets up, butts out their smokes, smooths out their garments, and gets into position. Once the music starts, each will begin to slow dance with an imaginary partner. Sometimes, when doing things like this, it helps to close your eyes, but hey, to each his own.

0.00–0.17

Miles Davis's "Flamenco Sketches," the final track from Kind of Blue, *begins to play. The light, already fairly warm, rainy-day-warm, gets even warmer, more dreamy.*

0.18–2.81

ONE

My father had a study upstairs in our old house. The smell of his American cigarettes filled its every nook and cranny, staining the books and records and the homemade green curtains. I secretly loved it. When I came home from school, before he came from work, I would creep inside this lonely room, play his favourite records, sit facing the window in his oversized leather chair with the oak trimmings along the edges of the armrests. One of them, the right-hand-side one, was scratched raw by our cat Howard until it became a much paler shade and felt worn and soft and warm like driftwood. The chair made a slight wheezing sound as it took the weight of my scrawny frame. And once I was settled in, I would run the fingers of my right hand along the oak trim and gaze outward at the view of our apple tree and our suburban neighbourhood expanding outward in a series of rectangular buildings and strips of fence behind it, everything divided up into quarter sections by the window's white painted frame. It would appear as though all the different houses were almost hanging from the branches of our tree, growing out from its extremities like miniature dollhouse Christmas ornaments.

. . . And then, after just enjoying that suburban calmness for a while, I would look at the cover of my father's dog-eared copy of *Kind of Blue*, at this handsome black man surrounded by the smoky darkness, slightly out of focus, with his slender nose, his mysterious pinky ring that caught the light just so, his eyes closed in some happy meditation, his lips pursed gently against his trumpet as though it was just the most natural place for lips to be. I tried to imagine how such sweet sounds came out of this configuration. I wondered who this man was, and if he lived in a house like ours with an American cigarette-scented room that almost nobody went into, an oversized leather chair, and an apple tree in the backyard.

2.82–3.26

TWO

I lost my memory once. This is years ago . . . The only thing that brought it back was looking out my mother's kitchen window while washing up supper dishes with her in merciful silence. And, later, playing an unfinished phrase from "My Cherie Amour" on the piano over and over and over and over and . . .

3.27–5.39

THREE

I had found the glove earlier that morning on the front steps of our apartment building, on my way out to run some errands. I knew it was his because I had seen him wearing it. It and the other one, of course. I had watched him from my window crossing the street on his way to our building. His last name is written in all-caps by his buzzer. I don't know his first name. He has a mole near his left clavicle, but you can only see it when he has his tie loosened and collar askew. He's a repeat traffic checker; he looks both ways not once but three times before and during his crossing and jerks slightly if he senses a driver getting impatient. He wears expensive shoes, but they don't always match his pants. His hair is thinning and the horizon of his cranium is an immaculate half-oval. He has permanent bags under his eyes, he tends to miss a spot while shaving, his cheekbones are broad as a clock's face, his jaw is almost square, and he is, well, beautiful. I take the glove up to his door and at the last minute before I am about to knock on it, I can hear a deeper silence fall inside his apartment. He's heard me coming down the hall and pauses whatever he's doing to wait and listen for a knock. He's playing a jazz record. I lift my hand. My wrist folds open like a book. I make a loose fist and notice my hand is sweating. But I don't knock. I close my eyes. My lips are parted. And the pause is eternal. I hear him hearing me. I know he won't come to the door unless I knock. A thousand years go by . . . And then, I gently place the glove on the floor before his door and, quietly as I can, I move back down the hall. Float really.

5.40–5.53

FOUR

I'd cry if I had to live way up in a high-rise. Nuh-uh. Where I live now, there's too many people below me as it is. And when I look out my second-storey window on my evenings off, I become every one of them for five minutes each. Five minutes. It can be very exhausting. Sometimes I fall asleep while I'm still one of them. Fuck, I hate that.

5.54–9.09

FIVE

I woke up, not with a start, just like I was meant to wake up at that *exact* moment. The clock said 4:44. Four, four, four . . . The stereo in the living room was on—but I never leave the stereo on. I looked at my dresser, my pants, my floor lamp. Everything was where it should be. Yet I sensed somehow that, while I was sleeping, all these things had been taken away somewhere and then replaced perfectly so I wouldn't notice. I know: it's crazy. I got out of bed and the floor was suspiciously warm. I put on my pants . . . In the living room, things looked equally fishy-and-yet-not-fishy. Everything was *exactly* where it should be and it was really freaking me out. But then I noticed the big change: the living room window was wide open, the green curtains billowing like shower curtains. The rain had stopped and now a pleasant, fresh-scented breeze was flowing into the room. It made me feel . . . kinda nice. I walked to the window and saw that a giant wooden hook was hanging there in front of it, just big enough to sit on comfortably. It wasn't windy so the hook was pretty still. I knew then that there was nothing to do but sit myself on it. I didn't do anything about the stereo; I just let it play. What the hell, I thought . . .

Getting out of my window was the hardest part; the edges hurt my foot and I figured it was best if I didn't look down, which made manoeuvering a little harder than it should have been. But when I got comfy on the hook, I looked around me and saw a bunch of these same giant hooks hanging in front of several windows in my building and in front of other buildings along my street. And other people, people I had seen before but couldn't tell you a single thing about them, they were all sitting on their hooks too. Some were just looking around like me; others were chatting with each other. One guy was passing around a flask of some sort; a rather nimble and attractive woman was using her hook like it was a trapeze; another two people across the street were playing Frisbee. Frisbee . . .

When the flask came my way, I thanked the person who handed it to me and took a sip. It was a good Scotch whisky: smoky but sharp. Is that a good way to describe Scotch whisky? Wait. Peaty? To be honest, it was maybe the third time

I ever drank the stuff. The moon was full and fat and wending through the clouds to say hello. The stereo kept playing the same song over and over. After a while, I couldn't tell where the song began and where it ended.

9.10–9.26

Sensing that the song has reached its end, each of the remaining dancers close their eyes, if they weren't doing so already, and all at once, they each begin to rise just slightly off the floor and hover there for a few drifting seconds, waiting for an ending that never quite comes.

Nancy
by Michael G. Wilmot

Although separated by generations, Alan and Jimmy find understanding, friendship, and common ground.

Nancy was performed as a staged reading as part of the Grand Theatre's PlayWrights Cabaret in London, Ontario.

CHARACTER LIST

Alan   An elderly man, eighties
Jimmy   A young boy, fifteen or sixteen
Passerby   An adult, male or female

...

Michael G. Wilmot spent a number of years on-air in radio before his love of theatre was sparked after being dragged to an audition to act as moral support for a friend. He didn't get that part but . . . he did get the next one! His writing has been mainly in the field of comedy, including writing freelance for *The Tonight Show with Jay Leno* and for Kevin Nealon during his stint on *Saturday Night Live*'s Weekend Update segment. As a playwright, Michael's works have been performed across Canada and the US, including successful productions at the Port Stanley Festival Theatre, Rainbow's Comedy Playhouse, and Globus Theatre as well as at festivals in New York City, Toronto, and London, England. Michael is a member of the Playwrights Guild of Canada and the Dramatists Guild of America and lives in London, Ontario, with his partner and fellow playwright, Lynda Martens. Visit him at www.wilmotscripts.com.

Nancy

Old man (ALAN) in his eighties is sitting on a park bench on a pleasantly warm spring afternoon. He is dressed neatly in a nondescript way. We see him occasionally nodding to people passing by as he unwraps a sandwich from a brown paper bag and begins to eat it. He tosses pieces on the ground for the squirrels. A skateboard comes rolling in from offstage and stops at his feet. He picks it up and examines it. A boy (JIMMY) of around fifteen or sixteen enters.

JIMMY   Do ya mind?

ALAN   Do I mind about what?

JIMMY   My board?

ALAN   Your "board"?

JIMMY   My *skate*board!

ALAN   Oh . . . is this yours?

JIMMY   Ya.

ALAN   Just about broke my ankle.

JIMMY   Doubt it.

ALAN   You do?

JIMMY	Huh?
ALAN	I asked if you really do doubt that it just about broke my ankle.
JIMMY	I dunno.
ALAN	Well if you did you'd be right. It just rolled up here and stopped. It's good to doubt sometimes.
JIMMY	*(pause)* You weird or something?
ALAN	Are you?
JIMMY	Am I what?
ALAN	Weird or something?
JIMMY	No.
ALAN	I thought you young guys wanted to be weird . . . to make us old guys feel even older. Isn't that why you have that stud stuck through your eyebrow?
JIMMY	No, that was just to piss off my old man. Can I have my board back now?
ALAN	Did it work?
JIMMY	What's it to you?
ALAN	Just interested that's all.
JIMMY	Why?
ALAN	Just to pass the time.
JIMMY	You *are* weird.
ALAN	Well, did it?
JIMMY	Asshole didn't even notice.
ALAN	I'll bet he did . . .
JIMMY	No . . . he woulda flipped. He's just an asshole.
ALAN	So, how many assholes in your family?
JIMMY	What?
ALAN	Is your mother an asshole?
JIMMY	No.

ALAN	Do you have any asshole brothers and sisters?
JIMMY	Are you like, senile or something?
ALAN	Well, do you?
JIMMY	No, it's just me and my mom. My asshole old man moved out last year.
ALAN	So you're a one-asshole family then.
JIMMY	*(smiling)* I'm gonna tell that to my mom, she'll like that. Hey, can I have my board?
ALAN	See all these little bits of bread I've spread around here?
JIMMY	What about my board?
ALAN	Just a minute . . . see these pieces of bread?
JIMMY	Yeah, so?
ALAN	If you're very patient and very quiet, the squirrels will come and take them. Then the next time if you put them a little closer, the squirrels come closer. Pretty soon they'll come right up and eat out of your hand.
JIMMY	I tried that once but they just ran away.
ALAN	That's because you weren't patient. You have to earn their trust . . . Look . . . there's a squirrel now! Sit down . . . slowly and be very still. *(JIMMY does so.)* Shhh, here he comes . . . don't move.

ALAN holds out a piece of bread. They wait very still and watch as the squirrel moves closer and takes it from ALAN's hand.

JIMMY	Took it right out of your hand! Cool!
ALAN	It's wonderful, isn't it? Feels wonderful.
JIMMY	What if it bites your finger?
ALAN	Nothing is without risk.
JIMMY	Whatever. You do this every day?
ALAN	Pretty much, if it's not raining.
JIMMY	What do you do, just sit here and feed squirrels?

That's pretty lame. I mean, unless they come right up to you like that.

ALAN   That's· what I like doing. But today, I'm also waiting for my wife.

JIMMY   She meeting you here?

ALAN   She'll find me.

JIMMY   So you're just sitting here? Why don't you go get her?

ALAN   Oh, she's with her friends. She wants me to wait for her. There are things you learn after being married for sixty-one years . . . one of them is when your wife wants you to do something, it's usually a pretty good idea to do it. And . . . there are times when you are going to have to be apart.

JIMMY   Ya I know, I can't see my chick all weekend. It really sucks.

ALAN   It usually does.

JIMMY   Gotta visit my old man. So I don't get to see her.

ALAN   You're right. That sucks.

JIMMY   Don't say that.

ALAN   Say what?

JIMMY   Sucks. Sounds gross when you say it.

ALAN   Point taken.

JIMMY   *(gesturing)* Hey, is that your wife over there?

ALAN   *(looking in the direction JIMMY is pointing)* No, no . . . she's much prettier than that . . . and her hair is pure white like an angel's. Besides, there was no flutter.

JIMMY   What do you mean.

ALAN   That little fluttery feeling I get in my chest when I see her. Don't you get that when you see "your chick"?

JIMMY   No, I get a woody.

ALAN	Ah, those were the days . . .
JIMMY	What?
ALAN	*(smiling)* Nothing!
JIMMY	Now I won't get to see her till Monday after school and that's like two whole days.
ALAN	As you said, that really . . . well, you know. When I was twenty, I didn't see my girl for almost three years.
JIMMY	Wow, what happened . . . you go to jail?
ALAN	No, no nothing like that. I went to Italy. With the Fifth Army.
JIMMY	The what?
ALAN	The Fifth Army. I joined the army and went to war. Seemed like a good idea at the time.
JIMMY	Oh wow . . . did you kill anybody? *(ALAN doesn't answer. JIMMY pauses.)* Did you?
ALAN	*(long pause, looks away, then quietly)* That was a long time ago.
JIMMY	Don't you remember?
ALAN	I can't forget.
JIMMY	So you're like one of those vets who came to my school and talked about the war.
ALAN	Yep.
JIMMY	*(uncomfortable pause . . . he's not sure how to say it)* Thanks.
ALAN	You're welcome.
JIMMY	*(happy to get back to a more comfortable subject)* So you didn't see your chick for three whole years? Man, I'd go mental.
ALAN	Maybe I did. We didn't have email in those days so we just had to write letters. Sometimes they wouldn't arrive and I didn't know what she was doing or how she was feeling or . . . anything. She

felt so far away. I didn't think it was possible to go to one place but leave your heart in another.

JIMMY   Ya sure, like you can do that.

ALAN   Yes, you can. Anyway . . . sorry . . . I'm boring you, you probably want to go ride your board. *(hands the skateboard back to JIMMY)*

JIMMY   I guess. *(pause)* You got the time?

ALAN   Nope.

JIMMY   Don't you old guys all wear watches?

ALAN   Nope. I've seen enough time fly by, I no longer need to check to see if it's still moving along. My schedule's pretty open these days.

JIMMY   It's just that my dad said I can't come back until five.

ALAN   Well around five, the sun should be just about touching that church steeple over there.

JIMMY   Sweet. You can tell the time by where the sun is?

ALAN   I can approximate it, yes.

JIMMY   What if it's cloudy?

ALAN   Then I just decide not to care what time it is.

JIMMY   Oh. So . . . how old are you anyway? Like, about a hundred?

ALAN   Close . . . eighty-six.

JIMMY   You're even older than my grandpa.

ALAN   And how old are you?

JIMMY   Fifteen. And I know how to drive, my dad taught me and lets me drive around the parking lot sometimes.

ALAN   Your dad?

JIMMY   Yeah.

ALAN   You mean, . . . the asshole.

JIMMY   I guess.

ALAN	So, kids don't wear watches these days?
JIMMY	I use my phone, but I forgot it at home. I'm gonna have like a million texts waiting for me. I gotta know what time it is or I'll go nuts . . . I might miss something.
ALAN	That's because all of your days are tomorrows. All mine are yesterdays.
JIMMY	That sucks.
ALAN	Not really. There were some good yesterdays. Some very good yesterdays. Like the day I met Nancy.
JIMMY	Who's Nancy?
ALAN	My wife. It was the first day of my second year at university and she was sitting across the horseshoe in my biology class. She had long dark hair and beautiful green eyes. She was looking down at her desk, then she raised her eyes, looked at me, and I knew she could see right inside me. She was across the room but I could feel her breath on my cheek. We looked at each other for a second, then I started to cry.
JIMMY	You mean, like a baby?
ALAN	No, there was just one tear, but I wiped it away hoping nobody noticed.
JIMMY	How come you married her if she made you cry?
ALAN	I married her *because* she made me cry.
JIMMY	Didn't she think you were a wussy?
ALAN	No. No, she didn't. Women are strange and complex creatures and one of the great joys in your life will be discovering that.
JIMMY	Why did you cry?
ALAN	Because she was so beautiful. Because she touched something inside me I didn't even know existed. And later . . . I cried because I loved her so much. She pushed the tears right out of my heart.

JIMMY	She what?
ALAN	She made me happy.
JIMMY	Oh. My chick never makes me cry.
ALAN	I know.
JIMMY	How do you know?
ALAN	Because if she did, you wouldn't call her "your chick."
JIMMY	No chick's ever gonna make me cry.
ALAN	It's not a bad thing. Really it isn't. Sometimes words can't describe the feeling . . . like when our son was born. I felt as if a part of my heart had been taken and put inside his little chest and both our hearts were beating with the same rhythm. As he lived, I lived. If he died, I would die. I'll bet your dad felt the same way when you were born.
JIMMY	Doubt it. He's weird, but not as weird as you. No offence.
ALAN	None taken.
JIMMY	Did you cry then too?
ALAN	We both did, Nancy and I. We just held each other. Held each other and cried. It was the best I'd ever felt.
JIMMY	That's totally weird. You cry a lot.
ALAN	I imagine it could seem that way. I really hope it happens to you. I hope you get to feel that.
JIMMY	I sure don't. Two grown-ups sitting there bawling. That's gross. Like I'm gonna let that happen.
ALAN	Well, if it does, you won't be able to stop it. Thank goodness. *(pause)* You'd better go, it's almost five. Besides *(his breath becoming laboured)* I think . . . I think Nancy will be here soon.
JIMMY	Ya, OK. Um . . . thanks for showing me the squirrels and stuff. See ya. *(starts to leave, then*

stops) Sorry 'bout calling you weird. It's cool you didn't get pissed at me. My old man probably would.

ALAN   I'm sure I do seem a little weird to you but you also seem a little weird to me. You're not "pissed" at me are you?

JIMMY   No. Actually, you're kinda cool. In a weird way.

ALAN   Thanks. Now, I really think you should be going.

JIMMY   Maybe I can come back tomorrow, or maybe next weekend, and we can get the squirrels to come back. (*JIMMY looks towards the church steeple and doesn't notice that ALAN's breathing is becoming ragged and he's holding his left arm.*) Hey, you're right, the sun is almost at the tip of the steeple! That's like pioneer time-telling or something! (*JIMMY then becomes preocccupied with retying his sneaker laces and doesn't notice that ALAN has slumped over on the bench.*) My old man bought me these skate shoes last time I was here, they're awesome. They're Tony Hawk shoes and you can only get them on the Internet. Everyone at school wants them . . . (*notices ALAN)* Hey, mister . . . you OK?

ALAN   I'm fine, you just go . . . go!

JIMMY   You don't look so good . . .

ALAN   The squirrels will still be here tomorrow, you can come back and . . . (*His voice is very weak.*) Just go, please. (*His eyes open.*) Nancy.

JIMMY   Oh shit, shit . . . want me to get some help? . . . sit up . . . sit up! Come on . . . don't do this, man . . . don't do this!! (*He tries to move ALAN to a sitting position, but it's obvious he's dead.*) Holy shit . . . no! Oh man!! Oh man oh man . . . (*tries CPR, but he doesn't know what he's doing)* Help!! Help!!

PASSERBY   (*runs up)* What's wrong?

JIMMY   (*almost frantic)* It's this old man . . . he just keeled over . . . shit, I don't even know his name!

PASSERBY   Oh my god, it's Alan! He's here every day. Here,

	help me loosen his shirt. What happened?!
JIMMY	I don't know . . . we were just talking and stuff and he fell over. You know him?
PASSERBY	Ya . . . Hang on, Alan, hang on . . . *(tries CPR)* Stay with me, Alan, stay with me . . . please, please! Come on, come on! *(to JIMMY)* Don't just stand there, call 911!
JIMMY	*(goes to his pocket)* Shit!! I don't have my phone!
PASSERBY	*(still trying CPR)* Come on, Alan, don't do this . . . *(to JIMMY)* Then go get somebody!
JIMMY	Who!? Who!? Oh god! Is he gonna be OK?
PASSERBY	*(listening to ALAN's chest and feeling for his pulse)* Never mind, never mind . . . he's gone.
JIMMY	*(upset)* What?
PASSERBY	We'd better go get someone.
JIMMY	No . . . no . . . oh man . . . he's really dead?
PASSERBY	Looks like it. . . . he said he had heart problems. OK, OK, you stay here, I'll get some help. I saw a cop across the street. *(starts to leave)*
JIMMY	Yeah, right. OK, but if you see a really old lady with really white hair coming this way, you have to stop her, don't let her see him!
PASSERBY	Why?
JIMMY	Because that'll be his wife! She can't see him like this! He said he was waiting for her.
PASSERBY	He told you that?
JIMMY	Yeah.
PASSERBY	Waiting for Nancy?
JIMMY	Yeah, that's her name.
PASSERBY	Nah, you must be wrong kid, Nancy died six months ago. *(leaves)*
JIMMY	*(calling after PASSERBY)* No . . . he said . . . he said she was coming. *(PASSERBY is gone, says this to himself)*

He said she knew where he was. He said he was
. . . waiting.

JIMMY sits on the bench beside ALAN. He looks shocked and confused.

As realization dawns on him he hugs his skateboard to his chest.

END

Burusera
by Laura Mullin and Chris Tolley

Two people become linked together by the most intimate of items: a pair of underwear. Welcome to the future, a world where every aspect of human connectivity is for sale to meet the needs and desires of sellers and buyers.

Burusera was commissioned by Watermark Theatre as part of their Canada 300 Series. It premiered in Rustico, PEI, with the following cast and creative team:

Maxx	Richard Beaune
Meesha	Malube
Man	Eloi Homier

Dramaturge	Erica Kopyto
Director	Robert Tsonos
Set Design	Jackie Chau
Lighting Design	Kirsten Watt
Costume Design	Laura Gardner
Composer	Boko Suzuki
Sound Design	Brian Kenny

CHARACTER LIST
Maxx
Meesha
Man
Voice (pre-recorded)

···

Chris Tolley and Laura Mullin are writers, directors, producers, and the co-artistic directors of Expect Theatre. Together they have created award-winning plays, installations, films, and podcasts that have engaged international audiences.

Their work has been nominated for five Dora Mavor Moore Awards in the General Theatre category and has been shortlisted twice for the Toronto Arts Foundation Awards. In 2006 both Laura and Chris won Harbourfront Centre's inaugural Fresh Ground commissioning award for the site-specific play, *STATIC*.

Notable works for the duo include *Romeo/Juliet REMIXED* (Toronto and Philadelphia), *STATIC* (World Stage), *AWAKE* (Next Stage Theatre Festival), the CBC Radio drama *The Tunnel Runners*, and the short film *AWAKE*, which made its North American premiere in Hollywood, California, and will travel to festivals across North America including in New York City and Miami.

Most recently, Chris and Laura launched PlayME, a national digital theatre dedicated to producing Canada's most innovative theatre works and short stories and distributing them globally via podcasts. To date, PlayMe has listeners in over forty countries around the world.

Chris lives in Toronto with his wife Dharini and daughter Olive. In 2015, Chris ran in the federal election as the Green Party candidate in the Toronto-Danforth riding, resulting in the best showing for the Green Party in the GTA and surrounding area and recognized nationally as one of the strongest campaigns of the 2015 election.

Laura resides in Toronto with her husband Craig and daughter Marin. She works as a freelance writer and has recently completed her play *ALLOWANCE* and her short story *History of Visual Sources*. Laura writes humour and parenting articles for the CBC.

Burusera

A single spotlight comes up revealing MEESHA, *an attractive woman in a short skirt standing stage right.*

MEESHA
: Do you want to look under my skirt? You know you do. You want to look, touch, sniff, taste. You want it all. Now. When it's warm, wet, and waiting. Just for you. You want my panties. And I want you to have them. Contact me now. Let's share this fantasy together.

Lights down on MEESHA, *lights up on stage left revealing* MAXX.

MAXX
: If you live alone, you're probably going to die alone. It's just a fact. And don't give me that, "Oh, no. That's never going to be me."

You have one fight with the wife, one death in the family—and boom, you're flying solo with nothing ahead of you but lonely afternoons listening to the dogs barking in your head.

That is—until fate comes to finally lift you out of your misery. An aneurysm. A heart attack. A stroke. And, poof—you drop.

You're gone. Now what happens? Nothing. Why?

Because no one's likely going to find you for months. Maybe years. You've become one of the lonely dead.

And it's my job to clean you up.

Lights down on MAXX. *Lights up on* MEESHA.

MEESHA   If you've been strapped for cash and done shit jobs to pay the bills, I'm going to bet you've fantasized about an easier way to make a quick buck. For those who have experienced truly desperate times, you might've even considered dabbling in a little light sex work.

But let me offer you another option. Nestled in the cozy grey area between "pornography" and "prostitution" exists another burgeoning business opportunity: selling your dirty underwear to strangers.

Now unlike me, you're probably too freaked at the thought of guys jacking off in your undies to make ends meet. So you'll stick to scrubbing toilets or fetching coffee instead.

Fact is—no one gets hurt. It's just underwear.

Now you're thinking—exactly how much money can one make selling used panties? Let me tell you this—I wish I had two vaginas.

I was searching job postings when I came across this guy asking for used underwear. He was willing to pay fifty credits a pair. I didn't give it a second thought. He wants schoolgirl panties. Done. A cheerleader? No problem. A naughty housewife? For five hundred credits—I tell him, I'll be anyone you want.

Now I've got enough clients to pay all my bills. Why stop? I literally do nothing except produce underwear. I charge per hour of wear, with a twelve-hour minimum. Extras are more, but for guys who like their skivvies pissed in, or worse … they can look elsewhere. I'm the boss of the deal. If anyone tries to fuck with me—I cut them off.

There are creeps. One guy wanted me to show up to a bar wearing the panties. I said no way. He went off saying I must be a "fat, hairy, disgusting guy." Project much, buddy? How do I know you're not a serial killer?

What I've come to learn is this: these guys don't just want undies. They want company. I don't think it's a stretch to suggest men who buy used panties aren't the most fulfilled people. The key is not to get attached. They have a need. I fill it. And I've made a pretty decent career of facilitating their darkest desires.

A ding followed by a disembodied voice is heard.

VOICE   You have one new Humanagram. *(pronounced Human-a-gram)*

Tight spotlight on MAXX.

MAXX   *(to MEESHA)* "Um, hi? I've never done this before, but I came across your ad and—"

MEESHA   Or your sister caught you sniffing her panties in the laundry room again. Spare me the bullshit. My time costs money.

Tight spotlight on MEESHA.

MAXX   "I want—I want to fucking cum all over your face while I hold you down and sniff your schoolgirl panties."

There is an awkward moment between them.

"Jesus! Did I just say that?"

MEESHA   "I'm sorry. I just provide the underwear."

MAXX   "Forget it. This was a seriously stupid idea—"

MEESHA   "But I *am* okay to hear your fantasies. We just don't meet in person."

MAXX   "My wife said my big mouth will always ruin the moment."

MEESHA   "Does your wife know you want to buy my panties?"

MAXX   "Since she moved out six months ago she doesn't care what I do."

Lights down on MEESHA. *Lights up on* MAXX.

I live in Toronto. Tens of millions call it home. The people who know I exist? You can count them on this hand. Sure. I meet new people at work every day. Only problem—they're dead.

When I first got in this business, things were different. That was before the Exit Button. You used to get your fair number of jumpers, hangers, slicers, ODs. Not like now. The Exit Button makes it easy, fast, painless. Fade to black. Over and out.

But you know what's weird? As dead as they are, I see more in their eyes than people I pass on the street. When was the last time someone said hello to you, or shook your hand, or gave you a real hug on your goddamn birthday? And that's kinda sad, considering if you're born today, you'll probably be celebrating one hundred fifty of them.

When people die alone, I find them sprawled on the floor beside crumpled laundry and dirty dishes, tucked beneath flowery bedspreads, or slouched against the wall. Months, even years have passed before anyone has noticed. Sometimes, all that's left are their bones. My wife used to say I had grown too comfortable with the job.

Between you and me, since she left there have been days when I've thought about fading to black . . .

He hovers his hand over his shoulder where his Exit Button is embedded.

It's not like I plan on using it. But I'm glad to know it's there.

He moves his hand away.

But then I sit down, have a vodka on the sky

deck, and listen to the city. And something tells me. I'm not alone.

Lights up on MEESHA.

MEESHA

After countless pairs of underwear sat on, slept in, and worked over, I was finally able to afford a condo of my own. I bought a hot one in the historic CN Tower district.

My first night there, I was unpacking boxes when I noticed my apartment's best feature: the view into my neighbours' private lives. I can clearly see into the towers across from mine. I see window after window of people in their units, oblivious they're in plain view. Most of them are alone, eating, sleeping, staring. I forgot about the boxes. I turned out the lights, and pulled up a chair to watch.

I don't usually have the chance to see my clients . . . *interact* . . . with my product, so when this new guy's order comes through with the address of 301 Front St., Toronto—I'm curious. His unit is on the eight hundred and ninth floor, directly across from mine. The zoom vision I've bought comes in handy.

The first morning he sleeps late and doesn't bother to get dressed. He sits in his living room littered with clothes and beer bottles, but it's otherwise empty. His wife must have taken all the good stuff. Then he curls up on the left side of his bed, and falls asleep. I watch him for hours.

The next day his first order arrives. White cotton low-rise panties. I zoom in to watch as he pulls out the package, carefully sealed for maximum freshness. I feel like Santa on Christmas morning waiting to watch him unwrap his new toy.

But as he takes the package out his hands start to shake. He throws the envelope down. He starts to pace. Keeping a keen eye on it. He stares at it. Like there's a fucking bomb inside.

I'm like—"Come on guy. You want this! Open it!" No. He pours himself a drink. Vodka. Then another. And just when I'm about to give up on him, he rips it open. Savagely tears into the panties. Inhales them like oxygen after being held underwater. Bingo! Customer satisfaction! Quality control confirmed!

But wait. Now he's on the floor. Trembling.

"Easy guy! They're pheromones. Not crack!"

She leans in for a closer look.

What's wrong with him? Is he crying?

"Hey buddy. Are you okay?"

Ding of an incoming Humanagram. Tight spotlight on MEESHA *and* MAXX.

MAXX	*(wiping tears)* "Hi."
MEESHA	"What's next? A cheeky panty, French lace, a Brazilian thong?"
MAXX	"I was thinking. Could we just talk?
MEESHA	"We're talking now."
MAXX	"I mean for real. Don't you want to just talk?"
MEESHA	"Isn't this more fun?"
MAXX	"You hear of those old Choose Your Own Adventure stories? My grandmother used to have them. You know the ones I mean?"
MEESHA	"You want to talk about old books?"
MAXX	"You would read the story. At a certain point you're faced with a choice. Turn this page to open a door. Turn this page to go down a hallway. One of the choices inevitably leads to the main character dying. The other leads to the next part of the story.
	Every day I feel like I'm in the most painful Choose Your Own Adventure story in the world."

He takes a moment.

MEESHA	"What is it?"
MAXX	"I'm worried."
MEESHA	"About what?"
MAXX	"My future. I was hoping you'd make it different."

MEESHA's *spotlight begins to flicker and some static sounds are heard.*

MAXX	"You still there?"

MEESHA's *voice starts to morph.*

MEESHA	"We're losing our connection."

MEESHA's *light snaps out.*

VOICE	This system has experienced a serious malfunction.

Regular light on MAXX.

MAXX	Have you ever owned a dog? Like a big dog—the kind you could put a child on and have them ride it to school. You're with your dog and you bump into a nice couple—guy and girl. What's the first thing the dog does? Goes straight to the woman and—whoop—his head goes up her skirt—nose in her crotch—sniffing, snorting, huffing, and his head pushes harder, nose digging deeper and deeper. You yell at the dog, the woman laughs but the dog just goes at it harder like he's digging for diamonds and it's making noises, and it's slobbering and the husband is thinking, "Fuck! That used to be my job!" Know what that dog was doing? Connecting. On a very deep level. With nothing but his nose, that dog knows everything about that woman. If she's pregnant, her cycle, how old she is—fuck—even what she had for breakfast. Why? Animal instinct. Connecting to others. Knowing them intimately. Inside and out.

Since my ex walked we haven't had any contact. But every day I imagine seeing her again.

He sees her.

And suddenly there she was. Sitting. Waiting for the bullet train. Her head turned away. Had she seen me too? I moved towards her. Slowly at first. But then I started to run. If I could just get to her. I push through the crowds. But then the train whooshed in. She stands up. Looks right past me.

Then this guy walks up to her. He wraps his arms around her. Kisses her. Holds her—just a second too long.

I knew what that creep was doing. I used to do that too. She would put a dab of scent, lavender. Right here on the nape of her neck. When I held her I could smell it. It was faint. But powerful. I scream—

Stop smelling my wife!

VOICE	You have a new Humanagram.

Lights up on MAXX *and* MEESHA.

MAXX	"I need to meet you!"
MEESHA	"You don't even know me."
MAXX	"No. But I want to."
MEESHA	"You know I can't do that."
MAXX	"You can't? Or you won't."
MEESHA	"I told you before. I don't meet buyers!"
MAXX	"Then I won't be one anymore! Please."
MEESHA	"Don't you get it? I'm just a fantasy."
MAXX	"You don't have to be."
MEESHA	"I know you're going through a tough time—"
MAXX	"That's not it."
MEESHA	"Guys think they have feelings—"
MAXX	"It's not in my head!"

MEESHA	"They think they develop a connection—"
MAXX	"You feel it too!"
MEESHA	"But it's not real!!!"

Beat.

MAXX	"I have to believe it is."
MEESHA	"Things are getting muddled."
MAXX	"Not for me."
MEESHA	"They're getting fuzzy."
MAXX	"Why?"
MEESHA	"I don't know!! Your wife left. You cry. The vodka—"
MAXX	"Vodka?"
MEESHA	"Yes."
MAXX	"I never told you that."
MEESHA	"No?"
MAXX	"No. How do you know?"

MEESHA *doesn't respond.*

"You're right. I don't know you. But I can feel you. When I'm home alone. You're there. That's more than I can say about anyone else. It's what stops me from hitting my fucking Exit Button. Someone out there knows I'm here. And you know what else?"

MEESHA	"What?"
MAXX	"I think you're lonely too."

Beat.

"And if I'm wrong. Well. I guess I really am alone. And there's nothing stopping me from hitting this anymore."

He places his hand on his shoulder, hovering over the button.

"What do you say? Should I push it?"

MEESHA does not speak.

"Okay. I guess that's it for me. Over and out. Fade to black."

He raises his hand to push it.

MEESHA   "WAIT!!!!"

MEESHA's light starts to flicker and goes out.

VOICE   You are experiencing a serious malfunction. Connection may be lost.

The static sound increases and MEESHA's voice begins to morph.

MEESHA/MAN   "You might not like me."

MAXX   "I'll take the chance."

MEESHA's light flickers back on, but standing in her place is now a MAN.

MAN   "Fact is—no one gets hurt. It's just underwear."

MAXX and MAN slowly turn towards each other. Three thunderous knocks are heard. On the last knock, light snaps to black.

Rebecca Burton has a BA in theatre and history from the University of Guelph, an MA in theatre history from the University of Victoria, and a PhD ABD from the University of Toronto's Centre for Drama, Theatre and Performance Studies. Rebecca has worked in theatre in various capacities: as an actor, collective creationist, director, dramaturge, playwright, stage manager, and technician. She also works as an arts administrator, editor, researcher, and educator, teaching theatre and literature. Currently, Rebecca is the Membership and Professional Contracts Manager at the Playwrights Guild of Canada, and the Lead Organizer of the Equity in Theatre (EIT) initiative.

First edition: October 2016
Printed and bound in Canada by Marquis Book Printing

Cover design and illustration by Patrick Gray

 **PLAYWRIGHTS
CANADA PRESS**

202-269 Richmond St. W.
Toronto, ON
M5V 1X1

416.703.0013
info@playwrightscanada.com
playwrightscanada.com